pieces of me

my diary of poetic life

t. marie

Reviews

Many would say that, *Pieces of Me: My Diary of Poetic Life*, is comparable to reading the diary of a woman who divulges her most intimate thoughts, secrets and life experiences. As a psychotherapist at a large Non-Profit Domestic Violence organizaation, I view this book much differently. The pages of the text are reminiscent of sitting in the back of a therapy room as a quiet observer. Reading T. Marie's passages of poetry and pages of self-discovery, is literally viewing ones individual breakthrough moments; as she connects the dots, patterns, and behaviors that have influenced her life and relationships with others. T. Marie takes you on an expedition of the heights and depths of her soul, fearlessly exclaiming that, although she is a child of God, she's not perfect. Readers are invited to challenge themselves, their beliefs, their own patterns of behavior..... allowing us to question, how might our own memoir read?

-Colleen Blackston, LGSW

This book is unlike anything I have ever read! T. Marie takes you through her lifeline of human interactions: some good, some bad, but relatable to anyone who reads it. She superbly recaptions every story into a poetic poem, which is nothing less than the icing on the cake! This is a stunning prelude!

-Joyeeta Stevenson
Founder of Kindred Spirits
Owner of Joyeeful Potions

As a spoken word artist, author, and proud feminist, 'Pieces of Me: My Diary of Poetic Life', tested more than just my mental faculties when reading her life altering autobiography. The literary body challenges the realms of individual self-expression, while conveying to the world that she is constantly striving, evolving and creating a more perfect version of herself. I would definitely recommend this book to women of all ages—ranging from teenager through adulthood. T. Marie's testimony, artistic ability, and bravery, are sure to embrace, inspire, and demonstrate what it means to be a woman, and artist, a mother, and a child of God, living in the 21st century.

-Journei, The Poet

About the Author.......

Instead of home on the range, I'm free, like a bird
A wingspan of an eagle flying around in my world
Unlike the traditional, a combination of various elements
To some individuals, my logic may not make much sense
Please do not attempt to criticize or conform my being
To suffocate and smother my style of everyday living
For I dance differently to the beat of my own drum
My National Anthem is more rhythmic than normally sung
The composition of my character is flavorful and spicy
Boredom cannot sit still around a spirit full of feisty
For those unable to understand, it's OK to let it be
Because after HIS creation, God broke the mold of "ME"
Delightful differences are truly a delicious addition
Which produce an unforgettable, savory sensation
No one should be identical or cloned in such a way
To where our world is occupied with just the unoriginal,
the dull and mundane
The imaginative and innovative also inhabit the earth

Possessing the creative ability to bring a new perspective to birth
Welcomed with open arms is how my uniqueness should be received
My pen of positivity is the purpose permanently residing within me

Introduction

A life-long expedition begins the moment we exit the womb! Our odyssey of the unknown is an exciting adventure; satiated with lessons that lead us to victory or a downward-spiraled defeat. Throughout my years on this earth I've treasured unbelievable joys, but have also tolerated many trials--- tempestuous situations that paused the productivity of my life.

For example, while in the midst of a marriage going awry, I prayed for spiritual guidance and sought solace and advice from my closest coupled confidants who had overcome obstacles within their union. Despite being counseled by professionals as well, remaining husband and wife was not an option or meant to be. I would soon be welcomed into the arms of single parenthood: an unfamiliar realm. I longed for a verbal or visual introduction of what I was about to embrace, however, I knew of no one holding that title. With God's guidance, strength, and the support of my family, we celebrate the success of my solitary status!

Although in life we travel as lone beings, all of us, at times, may proceed down the same path opting for diverse directions. The outcome of our choices will either be a help or a handicap. Regardless of positive or negative results, our occurrences can be shared with others; providing wisdom to the weary of what not to do, or bestowing the blessings of what to do. Either way, we all embody enlightening experiences to impart that will fortify and produce invincible individuals!

The poems you are about to read relate to everyday events: informed of, observed or involved encounters. A prelude provides the foundation of what inspired the writing. In spite of how personal or sensitive the subject, my intention from each entry is aimed towards inducing superlative strength and self-esteem, accompanied by an empowering spirit! I've noticed too many people put themselves in a position of degradation; depreciating their level of value by way of behaviors and actions. Other disabling factors, when outside forces happen to shift our rhythm, are throwing in the towel or resolving the matter in a "quick-fix" method that can potentially make matters worse. An additional crippling effect is when our mentality gauge is fixated on F, for failure, instead of V, for victor!

Whatever the ailment, we all have the ability to upgrade our lives to reach the pinnacle point of happiness, but it takes work. Just as a baby first learns to crawl before walking, we have to take one step at a time, one day at a time, to claim our prize! There were instances when I couldn't see clearly, for the fog of frustration and anger blinded my path, and poor decisions broke my stride to where I ended up falling. Nevertheless, I was determined to get back up! God provided the power, patience and perseverance I had prayed for. I'm just one of many who can witness and testify how awesome He is!

Not only am I a conqueror, so are you....you just may not realize it, yet. I do not claim to possess the answers or advice to ensure a euphoric existence, but I hope that my journey of journals can assist with your walk.

So, allow yourself to travel into My Diary of Life! I hope that a Piece of Me will ultimately bless all of you!

Marriage is a beautiful union-- one that I wanted to experience! My parents have been united for almost 50 years, so I was raised with a template of how it's supposed to be. To secure a successful matrimony, an individual must embody specific characteristics such as: patience, love, kindness, respect, truthfulness, and dedication. Although nobody's perfect (yes, that includes you), I felt that my spouse and I fit the criteria.

I met 'Jody' at church (just because you meet someone in God's house does not guarantee wedded bliss). He worked two jobs, lived independently, owned a vehicle and portrayed a soft-spoken, pleasant personality. He didn't possess the physical attributes I admire in a man. But as a matured Christian woman, I decided this would be the first time outward appearance should not persuade my decision. As we dated, I unearthed his inner traits of being one I could spend the rest of my life with....so I thought!

We exchanged vows in October of 1999. Within a year, we purchased a home and birthed a daughter. Some relatives viewed our choices as hastily made, but we were content with our determinations. I had previously expressed my want of two or more children, which I thought we both agreed on. However, Jody stated he was undergoing a vasectomy after our first child was born. The fact that he had one from a previous marriage resulted in him having two children. But the last time I checked, only one passed through my womb! As far as I was concerned, he committed premarital perjury; unbeknownst to me at the time, God had a plan!

Months after the baby was born, Jody's behavior went from happy pappy to hellish husband! I resigned from my employer; experiencing the joys and pains of stay-at-home motherhood. I retained responsibilities around the house as I doted on our daughter. Some might have deemed my new "employment" as effortless---it was far from it! In-between time, I purchased a home instructional course in hopes of acquiring a personal trainer's certification. I assumed study time would become increasingly available in the evenings when Jody came home; providing a peaceful reprieve. Nevertheless, a depressive despondence along with excessive entertainment claimed the remains of his days. He criticized my inability to use "free time" wisely. Jody felt deserving of coming home, eating dinner, and partaking of a ménage a trois: himself, the television and the couch! The three made love all night long until he retired to bed.

Petty arguments became a pattern as the years dragged on. I do not take kindly to being yelled at and spit on (regardless of accidental or intentional grounds), followed around the house with the baby in tow, blocking my path (I had to call the police), or raising a hand as if about to strike (I'll knock you upside your big head and think about heaven later)! Drowning in an tumultuous environment, I initiated a conversation to discuss the status of our relationship. I confessed feeling dispirited and detached; viewing him only as a roommate who provided DNA for a child. Spending time with the family was not his personal priority and our mutual communication was non-existent. I mentioned marriage counseling, but after three attempts with three different advisers, the results remained unsuccessful.

The final straw dealt with honor! A fellow member of the church made a pass at me after a drum lesson. 'Randy' was slated to sing a song in a couple of weeks and I had volunteered to substitute his place on the instrument. The two of us were practicing in the church by ourselves, and even though he had a reputation of being a "wanderer", I didn't feel threatened; he was aware of my marital status and was friends with Jody. In spite of that, it didn't stop him from kissing me on the cheek as we were about to leave. Immediately, he began to wrestle with me in a playful manner. I told him to stop but both of us, including coupons I was holding at the time, fell on the floor. He assisted in gathering them and extended his hand to help me up. Randy drew me close; attempting to kiss me, intimately. After pushing him away and retreating to my car, I sat in the parking lot....confused and upset. I contemplated approaching Jody about the incident; not because of their friendship, but of our dying marriage. I recounted the event a few days later. He seemed upset and promised he'd meet with Randy the upcoming Sunday.

I was scheduled to travel out of town with my mom, but felt assured he would handle his business.

I called Jody that evening to inquire about the inquisition. He feebly responded that Randy admitted to having inappropriate thoughts about me. I was baffled by the reply and Jody's acceptance of it. Regardless of the experience I endured, he basically believed Randy's account instead of his wife's detailed narrative. To make matters worse, despite my sitting or standing next to Jody in church, Randy would intentionally greet him individually. And one afternoon when I returned home from work, Randy was situated at my kitchen table while Jody prepared a meal for them to share. The absolute and outrageous disrespect he blatantly brandished pierced my heart and signaled the passing of our marriage. I moved out of the bedroom, inhabited the sofa bed and carefully calculated my Plan B....filing for divorce!

Our four year union I deemed a lie--- bamboozled by a person I thought I knew but never met. I shredded the wedding album...forbidding falsehoods to ever be viewed again! My "grieving process" did not consist of sadness but of infuriation; anger towards Jody for wasting my time and disappointment with myself for choosing him. The only prized possession: my one and only daughter (I later thanked God for having one child instead of the two I desired)!

Games were played on Jody's behalf during the divorce (his attorney was also inconsistent in attendance), the lawyer I retained seemed half-witted, but God was in control! With continual court dates pending after a couple of years I took a page from Tina Turner-- I kept my name and stated Jody could have whatever remained (which wasn't much). To me, peace was priceless! I wanted to rapidly rid myself of Mrs. and become a Ms.!

And on Friday, the 13th (My lucky day!) of January, 2006, my Declaration Day of Independence commenced!

D-DAY

This January day of mine
Predestined before my beginning of time
A long time coming, this day it was
Irreconcilable differences I deemed the cause

Year after year I tried to endure
For I'd never been in this situation before
A life of unhappiness I now lived
The mental and emotional abuse I hid

We had a child—for her, I tried
But didn't want my heart to go along for the ride
Unwilling to admit this is how marriage should be
I prepared for her and myself to be free

Investing and strengthening my mind, body and soul
Going back to school—so much I needed to know
Accepting and loving myself, and life
Now exiting a world full of strife

Initial attempts of knocking me down were feeble, at best
I recognized your evil as nothing but a test
After awhile your scandalous ways began penetrating
As your continuous Drama began to kill me softly

Smothered by suffocation, I gasped for air
If permanent changes weren't made I'd no longer be here
Digging deep within I'd have to step up to the plate
No longer allowing myself to be affected by your hate

You tried to Destroy me through word of mouth with lies
I could see the Destruction raging in your heart through your eyes
You tried to use my weakness—finances was the key
Briefly mesmerized by that carrot dangled in front of me

You kept it there as long as you could
But finally I recognized the game and understood
Your Desire to keep me at arm's length
To clutch, Deplete and Devour my strength

My eyes finally looked to the hills for help
I needed to talk to my Father, so I knelt
Asked for guidance, wisdom, clarity and peace
Maturity and resolution of these D- Days for me

You declared, "Just ask and it shall be given to you!"
As I continued to pray I felt brand new
Cleansed of the mess and Drama held within
Now nothing could stop me—I had Faith in Him

You told me you'd care for me day by day
Release the worldly possessions- give him his way
For no love is greater and I got your back
Not a thing in your life will you ever lack

If he wants to do wrong, that I will judge
Just make sure you live and do right—hold no grudge
My child needs a parent who has her best interest at heart
Don't worry about him, for today is your new start

T. Marie

Determined I am to pursue my Dream
I am following the Destination He Designed for me
I was blinded at first, but now I see

My D-Day is here
My D-Day is now

I'm free.........................

January 17, 2006

Back in what we call "the olden days" (1940-1960), marriage was considered a sanctified bond.... more so than our present era. Nowadays, divorces and dissolutions are on the rise and effortless to obtain; no longer deemed taboo, as in the past.

Women were encouraged to remain in a marriage--regardless of lovelessness, adultery, or other diverse complications. With most wives not working outside of the home, the ability to independently gain financial resources was challenging. Being solely dependent upon a husband could leave one feeling helpless and confined.

One of my older relatives offered advice during my marriage troubles. "Stay with him an additional five years to ensure partial receipt of his pension, which will help you later down the road." I instantly informed her that no dollar amount was worth wasting my life on a failed union!

She revealed hers was less than blissful, but was raised to weather all storms. Her spouse's unfaithfulness produced a son, whom I happened to meet for the very first time at my relative's husband's funeral. He looked like an exact replica of his father! Understandably displaying an uncomfortable stance, his attendance to pay respects showed undeniable strength and courage. Although they both sustained stares and hushed whispers, the pain from old memories resurfaced.

Despite their old-fashioned ways of life, I realized that some family members had my best interest at heart. They relied on what they knew to be sound advice, passed throughout the generations. Even though I appreciated their concerns, I trusted God was going to care for all of my needs. Accompanied with the pure adrenaline of determination to succeed, nothing was going to stop me from my destiny!

That's what I said, and that's what I did!

Some Said, I Say

Some said I wouldn't make it without having my husband
Some said I couldn't take it for I'd have no legs to stand on
Some said I had no chance as a single mother with a child
Some said to watch my dance, for now that I'm free, I could go wild
Some said since I'm alone that my life is over and done
Some said my heart would turn to stone

But they know not the rising of my sun....

I SAY I need no man to make it through my days

My confident and courageous attitude allows me to pave my ways

I SAY my stature is strong and able to withstand a fall

For I truly believe in me; proudly and powerfully walking tall

I SAY living a life of less will never come to pass

For my fortitude fuels a future of success that will forever last

Some said, but I SAY!

July 31, 2006

8

People can be unforgivingly judgemental; critically critiquing the most simplistic things: one's speech, walk, laugh....but most of all, appearance. My mom raised me with the saying, "If you don't have something nice to say, don't say anything at all!" Now, I'm not about to act self-righteous and behave as if I never cracked on anyone—that's far from the truth! But there's a vast difference between negative comments made in front of one's face, rather than behind their back.

During my brief marriage, 'Jody' and I attended a family gathering at one of his relative's houses. I recently had my hair styled in long, single braids. One of his sisters commented on how she liked it; inquired how long it took, what shop I went to, etc. Another relative quickly quipped her dislike of braids-- exclaiming that she would never wear her hair in that manner! The unwarranted remarks were shouted aloud during a moment of complete silence. During this awkward intermission, I wondered why an elder would behave so obnoxiously. Nevertheless, my knight in shining armor came to my rescue. No....not Jody; he never spoke up on my behalf. It was his grandfather, whom I adored! Paw-Paw asserted his enjoyment of my new look as I showered him with kisses. Even though one person's foolish comment was tasteless, he blessed my soul with tenderness!

After God created and formed each masterpiece, He broke the mold; none of us were designed to be duplicated (which eased my parent's minds). We all possess a variety of perceptions, imagination, creativity and originality. It's a beautiful thing when diversity, in every individual, can be appreciated instead of condemned!

Just Me

*You say you don't like the way I walk—even though
It was a gift from God, for He structured my bones*

*All my clothes aren't up to date or the latest trend
I've been showered with donations, so there's less for me to
spend*

*You tell me my braids are too ethnic and shouldn't be worn in the
workplace*

*With my head held high, I'm proud to display a symbol of my
heritage and race*

*I try to encourage others—lifting spirits up, when down
For no one desires to be alone when they need someone around*

*You complain my speech is too proper and I converse as if shades
lighter*

*However, articulating with dignity only makes my promising future,
brighter*

*You condemn and criticize when I miss a deadline regarding
personal goals*

Instead, find your own passion that will ignite your soul

*My laughter resounds heartily when enjoying comical life
It's daily medicine for my spirit and eases stress and strife*

You say I smile entirely too much and that it's sometimes blinding
My God has blessed me tremendously—so much, my light is shining

You despise that I eat right, exercise and care for my temple
But if you'd put down the knife and fork, for you it could be just
as simple

I'm personable in any audience whenever I take the stage
It's unacceptable to waste my life secluded in a solitary cage

You envy the gifts and talents God has bestowed unto me
Instead of hiding yours, choose to share them freely

God created you to be somebody—unlike me or anyone else
There's undiscovered treasure within—take time to investigate
your self

Implement the wealth that He has invested for you to use

And allow your focus to be upon no one other than, Just You

August 11, 2009

I wrote this poem while my beloved, Jalyn, was within her first three months of life. Being my first child, I made it of great importance to be available; a hands-on mom, like mine was. Informing 'Jody' of my desire and need to stay home and raise our daughter, I resigned from my employer. I wanted to establish an unbreakable bond and create a positive learning environment for my princess. Besides, the commanding prices for daycare would not burn our bank account. We did have to decrease our spending---purchasing only necessities---but from my standpoint, it was worth it! Jody continued working full-time, which provided medical benefits for the family, and within nine months I found part-time evening employment to provide additional income.

Regardless of frequent fatigue-filled mornings, the joy I felt waking my daughter--- seeing her smiling face, feet kicking with excitement and chirps of laughter---energized my emotions! Our days were never boring, for every dawning brought new experiences and adventures! I was blessed to hear Jalyn's first words, congratulate when she used the potty all by herself, hear her sing along with Elmo and his Sesame Street buddies and view her first steps. As far as I was concerned, those achievements belonged to the two of us; not to be divided amongst a babysitter.

Transformations became increasingly apparent as the months went by. Jalyn's strong will, leadership qualities, and characteristics developed at an early age. She would initiate expeditions within the playground areas, and was quick to the draw in raising her hand to answer questions in Sunday school class.

When I returned to full-time employment (amid divorce proceedings), three year-old Jalyn was sent to Aunt Mary's daycare; a close family friend who watched four other children in her home. All were around the same age and developed close relationships. Mary was an awesome teacher: loving and nurturing, educating the children about God and supplementing their foundation of ABC's and 123's. At age four, my precious ventured off to preschool. She cried the very first morning, but by the time I picked her up that afternoon, she was smiling and playing with the rest of the crew. Undetected, I proudly observed her exuberant independence while wondering what the future held for my baby.

Throughout the years, I've instilled good morals and values, including the importance of possessing a conquering spirit! Before Jalyn's first birthday, she was diagnosed with Neurofibroma Type I; an ailment where benign tumors form internally and externally. She underwent an unsuccessful brain surgery at the tender age of eight (a tumor formed too close to the brain stem to remove) and sustained chemotherapy treatments for about two years. Due to her condition, she was granted a dream trip to Hollywood, California, from the Make A Wish Foundation! Her many accomplishments include sashaying on the runway for a charity fashion show, volunteering her baking skills at a hospice center, an honor student and participant in her middle school's gifted and talented writing program. She was involved in the YMCA Teen Leadership class, a former star player on the YMCA's volleyball team, auditioned for a televised cooking show and starred in a summer camp production of 'The Wiz" as the lead character, Dorothy! Jalyn was even cast in her first high school play, "Aida", as a freshman. Her gifts and talents amaze me! Having endured her first surgery at two years-old, the strength and courage she has presented assures me that God has something wonderful in store for this brave, brawny and beautiful young lady's future!

Even though she is now a 15 year-old, hormonal teenager, I often reminisce on her younger years. We'll view the photo albums, listen to her babbling on a cassette tape recording and view her past videotapes (I know...seriously old school). Jalyn enjoys the sight of her animated appearances and I love expounding on the memories we shared back then. As we travel through the trials and triumphs of life, we continue to form special moments together... just the two of us! I'm blessed that God chose me to birth such a remarkable young lady. And no matter how old she may be, she will always and forever be my baby!

Always be my Baby

Each and every day I watch you grow
Your little hands and feet becoming large fingers and toes
No matter how big you get, you'll never be too grown
For you'll always be my Baby

Throughout the years your voice will change and mature
From cute and squeaky to confident and sure
You might even be taller than me one day
But it doesn't make a difference in any way
For you'll always be my Baby

Then soon you'll begin school, starting with the "pre"
A great time will be had, laughing and learning
With each passing grade you'll become smarter, too
And realize all the wonders life can offer you
It might be overwhelming but I'm by your side
Always and forever, with God as your guide
For you'll always be my Baby

As the years go by mistakes you will make
There will be risks and chances that you will have to take
Friends that will come and some that may go
But the ones that stick by you are friends for sure
Growing up, at first, might seem to be hard
Put your trust in God and you'll go far
Whatever you want to be in life, you can be
Stay determined and disciplined and you will achieve
Everything you desire and more
Who knows what life might have in store?

The President of the U.S. is a possibility
An astronaut or millionaire who owns properties
A Grammy-winning singer or professional athlete
A pediatrician or a podiatrist who works with feet
A scientist who discovers cures for diseases
A philanthropist who donates money for needs
A veterinarian who treats God's creatures
A loving teacher who educates and nurtures
A hardworking wife and mother who takes care of her family
A chef owning restaurants in multiple cities

But all of this is in the future, although not far away
So for now, let me enjoy these moments and say......

Each and every day I watch you grow
Your little hands and feet becoming large fingers and toes
No matter how big you get, you'll never be too grown
For you'll always be MY BABY!

12/23/2000

When becoming a parent, you are automatically thrust into an occupation without a manual or on the job training. Our parenting style is usually designed and formed from the foundation that was set while growing up. Even though I've never known of anyone perfecting this life-long assignment, I thank God He sent me to my mom and dad, for I was blessed with a phenomenal upbringing! I was exposed to a multitude of opportunities: piano lessons, art exhibits, sports, hilarious, unforgettable family trips, and moving to a better neighborhood at the age of five. While raised in a loving, respectful and nurturing home, I was shown and taught how to live a successful, independent life.

Now that I'm a parent, I possess my own rendition of rearing; occasionally delving into the archives of my childhood to retrieve some of the education I received. I have many responsibilities and ground to conquer as a single mother. I live the role of mom and dad—non stop! At times, situations arise: constructing repairs around the house, helping my daughter with her schoolwork, or playing the role of doctor. There are occasions when I need to stay home and care for her--to the extent of sacrificing what I desire to do. However, those circumstances automatically come with the prerequisites of parenting.

At any given moment, one must be able to morph into the role that is mandated. There's no justification for a lackadaisical or selfish sentiment. God entrusted us with His beautiful, small angels; to instruct, care for, love and victoriously prepare for every aspect of their lives.

Granted, parenting is not for everyone.... it can be a draining and tiresome task. Even so, I'm grateful I accepted this position, for it is truly the most rewarding career of my life!

Hat Collection

I have a collection of hats
Proudly on my head they're worn
Some to the point of no return
For they are well tattered and torn

Some I place as a tiara for a Queen
To inform those of my position
At times I am thoroughly appreciated
At times I receive no recognition

Every now and then I'm obligated
To unclog a sink or toilet
With my hardhat and tools, ready for action
There's nothing I cannot accomplish

A financial planner, planning for the future
Revealing the role of responsibility
Life coaching in decisive decision making
Teaching lessons whenever there's a need

Any time the name, Mommy, is called
Once again, ready to react
Whether a therapist one day, teacher the next
It's part of my single parent contract

To play the part that is presented me
No time to audition for
I transform into character necessary for the moment
Coming out, winning numerous awards

T. Marie

So many hats, so little time
But I'd do anything for my little girl
I may become exhausted in the process
But wouldn't trade a hat in for the world

January 14, 2009

I wrote 'The Art of Deceit' about a year prior to the events that occurred in this introduction. Even though I cannot recall what truly inspired me, the prelude provided presents itself correlative to the poem.

My job moved into an old jet-liner warehouse in 2007. Upon arrival, the structure already housed other office workers on the opposite side of the building. The employer wanted to consolidate numerous locations and corral its employees into one huge facility. With the need of saving money and the accessibility it provided in contacting other divisions of the company, I figured it was a good idea.

After a few months, our new residence was filled with many inhabitants; comparable to a brand new housing development. Rarely did I travel to the other side (which seemed like a two hour journey), but there were times when the need presented itself. During one of my expeditions I noticed a man walking down the hall: 6 feet tall, attractive and dressed nicely. I had to look back for a minute to confirm it wasn't a mirage, because that was the finest thang my eyes had encountered on the premises! I asked a few of my fellow co-workers if they knew who he was. No one knew his name, but I was determined to find out .. one way or another!

I didn't have to stay in suspense too long. I happened to be preparing to move and needed assistance with handling heavy equipment. I asked a fellow employee if she knew of any men I could consider without them getting the impression I wanted other items handled than just my furniture. 'Amarie' offered a list of names and answered with her opinion. She did suggest one guy: 'Jeremiah'. I had no idea who Jeremiah was until she described him and the location of where he worked in the building. My mystery man had been revealed! In order to establish contact, I sent him an email, naming Amarie as the reference, and proposed a time when we could meet in the break room.

We spoke for about five minutes regarding my need. He assured his availability to help, and made small talk as he walked me back to my unit. It was interesting to find out we had common acquaintances from our high school years, as well as his "knowing" of me through the grapevine. Before parting, he handed me his phone number saying to use it...anytime! When I called a few days later,

Jeremiah offered his aid with pre-moving tasks: packing, painting, etc. Basically, he was at my disposal. A month prior to the move, our relationship evolved. He provided breakfast for me at work, we took breaks simultaneously and scheduled play dates after hours. With two additional men lending a hand, the move was a success. Jeremiah and I continued to spend quality time together. However, during the third month of dating, behaviors began to change.

Gradually, Jeremiah became less available. I'm not trying to bestow the impression that a man has to be at my beck and call, but one can easily become accustomed to following an established schedule. On quite a few occasions he'd arrive at my house over an hour late; professing he was getting things together. Periodically, I'd discover him cornered in the hallways with various women he branded as only "friends". I attempted to believe him, but explanations and exhibits proved to be obscure.

Not long after the alterations, full-fledged issues erupted. I found out he had a peculiar relationship with a female co-worker of his. This mature woman began to badger him about our dating status. They had long, drawn out phone calls, including arguments at work and confrontations regarding their conclusion. The Young (or should I say, old?) and the Restless drama unfolding was a hot mess that I refused to participate in! Not only do I frown upon such nonsense, my hypothesis: for a female to be extremely riled up, to the point of making a scene, reveals continued contact between the two. Although he denied it, I let him know.....Ain't nobody got time for that!

After our separation, information concerning Jeremiah----such as the league of ladies he's entertained and various adult-themed activities----was forwarded. He still possesses adoration for fraternizing fellow employees, and due to numerous departments within the building, his pickings are plentiful.

The factors that failed our affair were being uninformed and unaware. Amarie knew him in a minute manner..meeting in a training class. If additional information about him and his ways were made known upfront, consent of our liaison would never have happened. After this disastrous romance, no longer will I have a honey where I make my money!

The Art of Deceit

I was your canvas...
Unused, Untouched
Unconscious of the talents you possessed

You portrayed yourself charismatically...
A magnetic charmer
Luring oblivious prey to your delightful duplicity

My nakedness, my naiveté'
Enticed you, Encouraged you
To create a portrait to your liking...
To my liking...

You fashioned your sketch
From a collaboration of antique repertoires
Accentuated with circular and linear abstractions

Your easel of alibis
Was the strength for your craft
Supporting your mounting mirages

So vivid, so glorious
So blinding were the colors
That blushed my bronzed frame

Each strategic stroke of your brush
Added another layer of lies
Unaware that your design was beginning to set
Becoming inevitably transparent.....

T. Marie

I stepped back to behold the wonder of your work...

A collage of confusion
Embracing sinister silhouettes
Fashion plates of fantasy
Induced illustrations of illusions....
Your murky mosaic became consciously clear......

I was your work of art...

I was your Masterpiece

November 21, 2006

About seven months preceding this poem, my manager designated 'Brianna' as our team's new supervisor. Even though she didn't possess previous experience in that role prior to her arrival, 'Darlene' thought she would be a valuable inclusion to our department. She couldn't have been more wrong!

There were times when Brianna would inquire about my work when all she had to do was read the conclusions I had transcribed on the claim. By choosing the lazy route instead of performing brief research, I wasted time explaining the "why's" and "how's" of specific resolutions. I informed Darlene that if Brianna would view a couple of documents, she'd be able to comprehend the outcome on her own; the statements were self-explanatory. In my opinion, she probably deemed some of her job duties as unnecessary. Other co-workers shared the same sentiment, in addition to voicing their concerns about Brianna's approach and disrespectful tone.

One particular day, our assistant manager took me by surprise. 'Sharon' charged towards my desk asking, "Where were you?!" I had no idea what she was talking about or meant by that question. After repeating herself, I responded that I had been at my desk. She proceeded to tell me that someone informed her I was out of my seat from 12:25 pm to 1:15 pm. Disciplinary actions can commence with that span of "absenteeism", so I promptly remarked that I was not gone that length of time. I asked who was the "somebody" making the claim. Sharon replied she could not reveal the source, which pissed me off to high heaven! I offered a discussion in the meeting room but she declined; retreating towards the direction of the room she originally exited. I had suspicions of who the culprit was, and lay in wait for her to reopen the door so I could view all who were inside.

One of my surrounding co-workers could not believe Sharon's approach, let alone the fact she did not reveal the instigator. I felt professionalism lacked in her advancement and Darlene should have been made aware of the situation, but was on her lunch break at the time. However, a few minutes later when she returned, I went into her office and asked to speak. As I turned around to close the door, another supervisor opened the one belonging to the room Sharon had originated from. Wouldn't you know it—there was Brianna! The visual only confirmed my wariness!

I conversed with my manager regarding the brewing mess. Considering Sharon's office was beside Darlene's, I spoke rather emphatically in hopes of her hearing my disappointment about the deceitful charges. Sharon knocked on the door as I was divulging the story of what transpired. She interrupted, stating since she was the one that received the information to allow her the opportunity to explain. Sharon provided her expository, claiming someone told her they had seen me outside. I interjected, contesting that I had not been outside and that tidbit had never been initially articulated. Next, she changed it up---I was out of the area from 12:25 pm to 1:15 pm, followed by the declaration of being discovered going through double doors. I looked at her with disbelief. Wondering why all of this was happening, I pondered for a moment. Recalling that I did enter double doors in order to go to upstairs, I offered an explanation. I briefed both ladies that a co-worker and I visited the credit union to withdraw money she owed for my daughter's cookie dough sale, but returned right away.

Darlene said I could leave after my testimony. Sharon quickly added that I should have apprised my supervisor of where I was going (which provided verbal proof Brianna inaugurated the chaos). I shook my head in disgust and closed the door behind me. I was outraged that Brianna had the audacity and ability to create an unnecessary stir!

I was called into Darlene's office later that afternoon. She explained her problem with the fact that no one made a case about the co-worker who accompanied me. Since there was not an issue made against the other female, why was there one made against me? I appreciated her fairness and clarified my displeasure of being incriminated for things I had not done. I inquired, "So, all we have to do now is blurt out blasphemy and that individual will immediately be at fault? No one should possess that kind of power!" She agreed the occurrence was unfair. I told her that if I have another issue of this magnitude, I will take the matter to a higher authority.

To this day, Brianna remains my supervisor. I refuse to request a replacement; she will have to endure me and vice versa. I can address her in a civil manner, but our working relationship is unrepairable. I do not trust nor have respect for her, or any person, who would intentionally attempt to inflict harm--whether physical, or in this case, my livelihood. I view her as a miserable person searching to strike down those who are happy, joyful and content. But what she doesn't realize is that I'm way too blessed to surrender to her stress!!!

QUEEN OF CONTEMPT

You're crass, mean-spirited and full of anger

Coming to work, spreading your cancer

A title you hold to where others look to you

But displeasure you receive with your bad attitude

Sneaky and slithering your way around the office

To entrap and devour all that brings you grief

Your repugnant reputation precedes you

The horrid stench of your verbalization

Displays you as a damning diva

Ready to render execution of expletives at a moment's notice

Very deceiving, with your cunning smile

You settle on your throne with your head held high

Demanding praise from your bamboozled subjects

ALL HAIL THE QUEEN "B"!

December 26, 2012

I long to become the type of person who excitedly anticipates rising every morning to go to work! However, at the time of this entry, I haven't yet reached that destination. Don't get me wrong—it is a blessing to even have a job in our present economic time, but it's not the type of occupation where I feel I belong... where I'm destined to be. In addition, with the position I currently hold, I am subject to endure difficult, temperamental individuals and interact with people whose names would not be inscribed on my list of favorites.

In the poem, Queen of Contempt, I thoroughly describe my supervisor's character, reputation and feelings towards her. Furthermore, it seems as if I still attend high school due to the immature behavior that's prevalent and accepted from our superiors. A combination of those ingredients guarantees a recipe for job dissatisfaction! Day after day, reflections regarding my profession have drained me to the point of feeling exasperated. Although a hiring freeze has been executed, I continually explore new employment opportunities at various locations within the company.

In the meantime, I came to the realization that a change is going to have to transpire.....starting with me! Our thoughts are extremely powerful and dictate our mind-set, which in turn direct our moods, decisions, outlook, and so forth. If I commit to consistently possess dismal thoughts every day before, during and after work, it will consume my consciousness and eat away at my entire being--- like an acidic substance I chose to change the dial my thoughts were fixated on to things of a positive nature instead of deeply drowning in the negative. When that happened, I saw everything around me in a new light, became increasingly appreciative and grateful for what I do have, and concluded that God placed me at this job for a reason. Regardless of the rationale, I have to represent Him to the best of my ability. It all begins with changing my focus!

MENTAL DIAL

From Monday through Friday I awake to find
A cloudy, negative mist form in my mind
A fog-like haze, settling around and about
Instead of a good morning smile, I protrude a heavy pout
No desire to prepare for where I must attend
For 8.5 hours I feel there is no end
Performing work for others while others perform no work
Surrounding myself with liars, cliques, heifers and jerks
The only way I can escape this monstrosity
Is to shift it all around and think positively

So.............

From Monday through Friday I awake to find
The blessings of God form in my mind
How He allowed me to awake to see another day
As I greet myself in the bathroom mirror with a smile on my face
Preparing to attend my 8.5 hour grind
I'm thankful I can make the bacon to put in the pan to fry
Working to full potential, I perform that ability
With considerate co-workers imitating alongside of me
I have the capacity to modify my mentality
Over-riding the negative with positivity
Keeping my focus focused away from captivity
A change in my mental dial will truly set me free

January 3, 2013

I don't know what prompted me to write this poem, for I've never experienced physical abuse, thank God! Unfortunately, I do know some women who have. It didn't end tragically but sufficient damage was sustained.

I remember when a friend of mine was dating 'Chad' (her boyfriend at the time). From the very beginning of their relationship he possessed characteristics of a controlling nature: frequently calling and demanding she answer, regardless of where she was or might be doing. Chad was extensively insecure; berating 'Jillian' if she was unable to accept his phone calls before they went to voice mail or arriving home later than the usual time. I had presented my opinions and perceptions concerning her new found love. Although Jillian heard me and appreciated my apprehension, I felt as if an impenetrable blockade obstructed my words from reaching its destination. Regrettably, the verbal, emotional and mental abuse did not prevent her from marrying him. Physical abuse has filtered Into their three year union; producing visible bruises, scars and confusion. Jillian's actions of remaining in the marriage contradict her words of the desire to retreat----unable to tolerate the violence yet unwilling to terminate her vows.

Domestic abuse is running rampant throughout the world! Murder-suicides are becoming commonplace and occurring at an astounding rate. Statistics show that every 9 seconds a woman is battered in the United States; 4.8 million American women experience a serious assault by a partner during an average 12 month period, and more than 3 women are murdered at the hands of their husbands or boyfriends every day.

A question looms upon us---Why do women stay in abusive relationships? You have some who confess undying love for their partner; accepting apologies of, "It will never happen again." Other individuals are too afraid to leave for various reasons: He'll take the kids...I know he truly loves me..I can't make it on my own...He'll kill me if I ever try to leave. For those who were raised in a household where abuse was the norm, generally the cycle continues to repeat itself, generation after generation. The suffering needs to cease!

Women, regard yourselves as the Queen you are! Enduring cruelty may not physically wound or kill you, but it will definitely destroy your spirit, douse you with self-doubt and deplete your inner strength; prohibiting wisdom and the willpower to escape. Mothers, think of the observing effects it will have on your children. Would you want them to grow up and turn into an abuser (boys who witness domestic violence in their own home are three times more likely to become batterers), let alone, be abused (40-60 percent of men who abuse women also abuse children)?

Numerous agencies will welcomingly assist you in various types of abuse situations: counseling, someone to talk to, or providing immediate shelter. Don't surrender for the gift-giving, sympathetic approach. It's only temporary until the next episode. The longer you continue to reside in an abusive relationship decreases your chance of survival.

The next time you're in front of a mirror take a good look at yourself. God doesn't make junk—He made you a priceless jewel!!!

Aren't you worth living?

National Domestic Violence Hotline: 800-799-SAFE (7233)
                                       800-787-3224 (TTY)

Rape, Abuse & Incest Network   800-656-HOPE (4673)

30

TORMENTED LOVE...

The rampage just ended with a blow to my head
Why does it seem this hate he demonstrates is love instead?
A punch to the mouth replaces kisses on the lips
Instead of arms embracing the exchange is with fists
I know not the reason, I can't tell you why
But I see the ignition within the darkness of his eyes
Once so loving when proclaiming to God his vows
Once living in heaven but enduring hell now
Screams in my face, demeaning my spirit and soul
How much more can I take? I really don't know
Part of me exists in this world I'm accustomed to
Part of me wants to leave and start a life anew
After the attacks are over begins the romance
The flowers, the "I'm sorry's", the same song and dance
The illusions only last for a short period of time
Then the story is paused and set back on rewind
Over five years this is how my life has played out
Does my husband love me? Oh yes, without a doubt
He told me numerous times, though in destructive ways
So I tolerated, hoping that one day soon things would change
And that day has come—it's finally here
No more having to live my life in extreme fear
If I would have left sooner I might have survived
But I let his "love" kill me...·For I have just died...··

April 2, 2007

31

Gone are the times when we lived in a moral and value-filled world. It's extremely rare for people to abstain and initiate sexual relations on their wedding night. Instead, many opt to perform a "test drive" before committing to purchase, which can prove to be a costly mistake.

I remember the day: November 7th, 1991. Earvin "Magic" Johnson (former Los Angeles Lakers star) announced his retirement from basketball due to the revelation of having contracted HIV (human immunodeficiency virus). He was notified after receiving blood test results from a routine medical examination. The world was stunned hearing the news! At the time, HIV was deemed a contagion for homosexuals or intravenous drug users with unsanitary needles; not a congenial man with an infamous, infectious smile and personality.

It was a sad situation. Headlines depicted sexual promiscuity and conquests with groupies, alongside claims from a former best friend doubting his sexual preference. Concerns if his wife and children had contracted the virus were of the utmost priority. To everyone's relief, they were tested and found to be negative. Although Magic was fighting his battle, he also brought forth a blessing; a heightened awareness and education concerning HIV and AIDS (acquired immune deficiency syndrome), but only for the individuals who were sincerely listening and learning.

I commented to my parents that people would probably return to their nonchalant sexual behaviors within a year. Sure, it was frightening the moment Magic exposed his life-altering circumstances. But sooner or later, the crises would creep towards the back of people's minds. Presently, folks are using their "friends with benefits" packages under the assumption that it's safer to claim one person as their designated driver. However, that person had friends before them, and so on. Unless a monogamous couple are exempt from a past sexual history, both are at risk of inheriting an STD (sexual transmissible disease), such as herpes, syphilis, gonorrhea, or something much more destructive. HIV can reside in your body for quite some time. Within 10 years, about half of the people whose HIV is left untreated become ill and develop AIDS.

An internet statistical report (last updated July 2015) on the amFar website (The Foundation for Aids Research) stated that nearly 37 million people now live with HIV. In 2014, an estimated 2 million people were newly affected, while that same year, 1.2 million died from AIDS. Astonishing news regarding our youth: 2.6 million who now live with HIV/AIDS are under the age of 15!

Regardless of sex being a beautiful, bonding experience between a man and a woman, it can also be a death sentence. Society has portrayed it as an extra-curricular, gratifying activity—not what it was truly intended for: the anticipated expression of love between newly married couples on their wedding night.

HIV/AIDS is a non-discriminatory illness, which can strike anyone at any vulnerable and unprotected time. It's impossible to believe that everyone will abstain, and in no way am I condoning individuals to partake in pre-marital pleasure. But practicing and preaching the benefits of safe sex can potentially safe someone's life.

The more knowledge you receive, the wiser your choices will be!

Uninvited Guest

I am welcomed inside, sometimes no questions asked
Although you cannot see me, I enter unmasked
My companions have shown me the entrance to your door
I do have choices of access, for there are two more
Places to lay my head down and take a rest
Where I can enjoy the warmth and comfort, at best
I allow my friends to have pleasure just for awhile
But soon I'll appear with a cunning, devious smile
First I move about the party with a little conversation
Then maneuver to the dance floor for plenty of penetration
As bodies interlock and souls intertwine
I now take full possession and claim you as mine
You might not think I'm there for looks can be deceiving
But you cannot deny me residence in your blood stream
For I'll pillage your immunity and plunder your life
Kill your dreams of becoming a husband or wife
Have children—go ahead—if it's worth the risk to take
But all of this could be prevented by the decisions you make
Be sure you wrap your gifts before you invite my friends
For I can follow, gain entry, and steal your presents in the end
Your party may be over, but not entirely
Forever your guest of honor, inseparable, just you and me......

December 27, 2008

When working full-time outside of the home, fellow employees have the ability to become a second family. Although completing tasks is crucial to maintaining employment, our personal lives have a way of infiltrating into our routine. Whether it's the excitement of a new romance, a death in the family, drama involving our children or returning from a week- long vacation, we desire to communicate with people we are continuously connected to.

I've cautioned folks on reviewing what is about to be said before releasing private details. The selection of the intended party is crucial, for some individuals' lips are unlimitedly loose and cannot permanently secure top secret information. Usually, I am wary of disclosing confidential business, but a simple answer found me questioning a treasured friendship.

During a follow-up neurology appointment in 2008, I was notified of a tumor located at the base of my daughter's brain. The doctor wanted to perform surgery within a few weeks. Until that day arrived, additional medical appointments required our presence. Being the super, single parent (and the only one possessing medical insurance for my daughter), I accompanied my baby to every visit; sometimes unable to receive compensation due to exhausting all of my sick, vacation and personal time from work. FMLA was a safety net, but the inability to accrue financial gain put a slight strain on my bank account. My supervisor, 'Renee', sympathized with my situation by allowing me to work over in order to receive full pay, which was truly a blessing! I was scheduled to be off three weeks for Jalyn's surgery and recovery period, and the potential loss of wages during that span of time would have been burdensome.

One week prior to the operation, I worked an additional hour every day to supplement hours I had missed for a doctor visit. 'Troi', a co-worker and friend (assigned to a different unit but positioned in the same area), asked why I was staying later than usual. I explained the circumstances to her without a care in the world. Surely she would understand the reasoning behind my laborious mindset: preparing for my daughter's surgery.

A few weeks after returning, Renee, along with her boss, 'Stephanie', summoned me. They inquired if I had previously mentioned to Troi about working over, which I admitted to. Both ladies began to advise me regarding my business—be careful of betrayers! Curiously confused, I asked for an explanation about the sudden warning. Apparently, Troi wanted to work over in hopes of securing time off for an upcoming vacation. Stephanie managed the departments in our section and informed her she was unable to do so due to the rules, policies and procedures of our handbook. Troi retaliated with her words; denouncing her disapproval of their consenting my identical request. However, our situations were of a diverse nature.

Stunned and disappointed, I approached my friend and demanded the motive for bringing my name up during her dispute. She professed her innocence, but I recalled a prior incident when she had dropped names in order to plead a different case. Due to our close relationship--having met and fellowshipped with each other's families--never would I have thought she'd expose my genuine justification as grounds to help her cause.

After healing from the backstabbing pain, I formulated a new plan: no longer would I allow co-workers into my life outside of work. It was extremely difficult to accomplish. Excluding others can lead to a very lonely existence, but beautiful bonds are created when participating and sharing in one another's lives. So six months following my flight of being a companionable co-worker, I decided to embrace my employer relations. I missed the camaraderie, the comic relief and the conversing. Slowly, I allowed my heart to soften-- delving into developing deeper friendships while gingerly guarding my steps.

One never knows what information can be used against them, so be aware and attentive of your words and actions. Precautions can prevent a breach of your personal business from going public.

BUSY BODY

Your body is busy
Tryin' to crack my business code
Asking others for the combination to my safe
Not many are inclined with the encryption
That's privileged and confidential....
You continually sniff around for a credible scent
Your snoopin' puts a dog to shame
Searching for a crack or crevice
Of any obtainable information
Searching for an opening or outlet
To slither your way into my world
To hack my files and retrieve data
And retreat to your hideout
To reveal your latest findings
But fortune you shall not find
For my security system is...
Unbreakable, Unshakable
Indestructible, Unreachable
So abort from your cruel intentions
And keep your body busy
With your own business!!!!!

June 28, 2007

Being that this book is about various elements of my life, I feel the need to divulge and expose myself with the utmost honesty. We all have fallen short at times, which is an expected estimation----no one is perfect. We've committed acts that we'd love to lock up and throw away the key to. Negative circumstances, shared between us and God, we desire to take to the grave; never to be unearthed or discovered. Due to the distressful events endured, I've dreaded writing this intro/poem. Nevertheless, I had to remember that what I might aspire to maintain in secrecy could actually be someone's saving grace!

In my early twenties, I found myself in a serious situation.......I became pregnant! Despite recklessness during the intimacy, I was aware of precautions (birth control methods) that should have been implemented. First and foremost, I should have practiced abstinence, for 'Stephen' wasn't someone I loved or even cared about. Not only did I treat our encounter as a recreational activity, I was convinced that IT would never happen to me; deceived by my own self-proclaimed invincibility.

Regardless of a positive pregnancy test, I encompassed my world with denial. For a couple of months I failed to show any obvious signs of physical changes, which allowed my mentality to continue the regular scheduled programming of an undisturbed life. By the end of the first tri-mester, a slight baby bump greeted me every morning. Attempting to camouflage my shame, sweatshirts provided protection---in more ways than just the cold weather outside.

Panic appeared as the weeks went by. One would wonder why I failed to inform my parents of my predicament. Even though their love for me was unyielding, I envisioned their extreme disappointment. Predicting their probable expressions of pity, accompanied with thoughts of being the daughter wearing the "scarlet letter", I chose to take matters into my own hands.

Although I did not embrace abortion, I arranged to become my own assassin. In hopes of a miscarriage by way of malnourishment, meals consisted of a small piece of fruit followed by numerous diet pills. My unsuccessful solution drove me to partake a more drastic action: laying face down, forcibly pounding my expanding belly on the floor.

Conducted three to four times a day, I was confident that nature would eventually eradicate the issue. To no avail, the baby remained.

Surrendering to what I deemed my last resort, I spoke with Stephen and demanded half of the cost for an abortion, however, he refused! Not due to disbelief or lack of funds but he wanted the baby---he was against my resolution. Though contradicting, I admitted to opposing these measures until now, since my "remedies" had failed. Desperately seeking a center, I found a place 70 miles away that accepted patients up to 22 weeks. I was 20 weeks along on the day of my appointment.

Upon arrival, I was greeted by protestors surrounding the clinic. I happened to make time for one lady to spew a 30-second plea---reinforcing what I believed to be true---that I was about to kill a baby. She encouraged a change of heart, while handing me a flier that depicted drawings of a partial-birth abortion. The pictures showed a live baby extracted from the womb, with a sharp instrument puncturing the back of the baby's head. The brain was suctioned, causing the skull to collapse and death to follow. I froze-- unable to move---until one of the workers at the Women's Center rushed from the building to guide me inside; ensuring potential dollar signs did not retreat with second thoughts.

I sat with a counselor who explained the process, but not as explicitly as the pamphlet presented. Numerous rods would be inserted inside to promote dilation of my cervix. This would occur for two days (the clinic had their patients stay in a hotel down the road for convenient access), and on the third day the final task would take place. Immediately after her "welcome", I was ushered into the doctor's office for the first step to be performed. After being instructed of the time to return the following day for a repetitious visit, I traveled to my temporary residence.

Due to conversing with my parents on a daily basis, disruption of our routine had to be prevented, for they had no knowledge of my whereabouts. So, while stewing in a numb-like disbelief of my pre-meditated plan, I reached deep within to portray an Oscar winning performance of a daughter who was doing just fine. After "fooling" them, I struggled to do the same with myself. Brainwashing thoughts of, 'I'm doing the right thing', repelled every fiber of my being. The next day, concluding the implementation of fresh rods, I returned to the hotel room and wrote a letter to my mom and dad, narrating the origin of my odyssey; when I first encountered Stephen to the current crime I was about to commit. Their letter would be delivered once I returned home.

The next morning I struggled to open my eyes; I knew what the day was about to bring. In between the panic and pangs of labor, I drove the green mile down the street to the death chamber. In spite of the upcoming "delivery", the nurse's nurturing words and inquisitive compassion of my physical welfare fell on deaf ears. When the doctor arrived to examine how far I had dilated, he commented that I'd be ready to go in less than half an hour. Enveloped with doubt, I questioned....was I making the right decision? Was it too late to back out? Was I going to hell for this when I died? The 30 minutes of isolation had my mind spinning out of control!

When the nurse returned, she took my hand and escorted me to a bigger room containing the murder weapon: the suction machine. I was directed to lay down and the doctor would be in shortly. While anxiously waiting, a shrilled scream came from down the hall. The pitch rang throughout my entire body, as if an alarm awakening me from a nightmare! Wide-eyed with fear, the nurse tended to my uneasiness by calmly assuring I was making the right decision, along with the normalcy of my feelings. After concluding her speech and checking my vitals, 'Dr. Deathblow' entered the room. Apathetically, he recited his presentation while my feet were placed into stirrups.

"I changed my mind! I changed my mind!" I shouted, but no words parted my lips. I was immovable and drowning in an indescribable atmosphere! Pressure was overwhelming in my lower region as my baby, along with my heart, were being removed. The sucking sounds made me want to holler aloud! An oxygen mask was placed over my face, muffling and silencing tears of a tortured soul. Sobs of shame were whimpered as I felt my baby leave its nest. "Cut the umbilical cord," the doctor ordered. Then, it was done---in more ways than one. Not wanting to accept my role as an accomplice, I released myself into the universe........reconnecting upon discharge from the facility.

I cried a river by the time I returned home, and dropped the letter off at my parent's house. They were devastated, but their love for me remained and I was forgiven. Remorsefully ridden with guilt, I had the hardest time forgiving myself. I prayed consistently for God's forgiveness, even though He already had. Audible apologies filled my apartment on a daily basis; tears drenched the pillows and horrific memories of the days prior consumed my entirety. It wasn't until I begged my baby to forgive me---to exonerate my self-centered, immoral behavior and actions---that the healing process began. The warming touch of love, the whisper of mercifulness and covering of compassion, slowly pieced my brokenness back together. The journey was a trying one! While writing this introduction I still shed some tears, but have accepted and professed my wrongs to God, repented for my sin and am speaking out; hoping to prevent others from traveling the same path or to those who find themselves in a similar circumstance at this time.

Scientists might persuade you to believe that abortion is not killing a baby because it has not developed enough to sustain life on its own outside the womb. But, should that matter? For example, while in the process of baking a pie, we deem it a pie. I've never heard anyone claim that they have eggs, flour, sugar, butter, fruit, etc., in the oven---it's called a pie before it's fully cooked. When planting flowers for a garden, most people don't convey they're planting seeds in hopes of growing flowers; plainly stated, they're planting flowers--speaking on what's to become when fully mature. How disturbing that we can affirm frivolous "things" have reached fruition when in the stage of incompleteness, and go to war while attempting to decipher when a baby should be revered as a human life! Just as a planted seed evolves---receiving nourishment from water, sun and fertilizer---so does the seed of life planted within the womb.

From my experience, I pray that I've educated someone....changed the mind of one individual in believing, without a doubt, abortion is not the right choice. There are various alternatives: keeping the baby, temporary foster care (or with relatives) and even adoption. Whatever your recourse, I urge you to choose life! Just remember.... if you're reading this, SOMEONE CHOSE YOU!!!

Acquitted Execution

I regretted having you leave, the moment I let you go
An opportunity to change my life
Dismissed at the thought of an inconvenience
Your presence, inconsistently welcomed
Your absence, remorsefully empty
What could have been, should have been....
I allowed you not to be
Having the possibility to bless others
I cursed with a signature
Permission granted to withdraw pending parenthood
The intertwining of our body and soul
Suctioned and extracted instantaneously
The physical pain of removal overwhelmed me
The emotional pang of grief attacked my heart
The mental anguish of a selfish slaughter
The spiritual disconnect left me solitarily confined
Inevitable death I housed within my womb
Granted me a second chance at living
Rescued from the melancholic quicksand
A small Angel forgave my destructive decision
Speaking love in-between mournful pleas of pity
Drying the tears that flooded my gates
Resting in the glow of compassion
No longer imprisoned by my immorality

But if time could rewind....I'd choose LIFE!

May 5, 2015

Due to the fact I work with so many women, it's not uncommon for us to talk amongst each other about our problems and issues——particularly in the realm of men. Some of us are able to discuss our dates without reciting every detail, while others savor their self-proclaimed stardom.

'Mary' was known for announcing an overwhelming amount of personal business to the office gossips and yet, time after time, would question why our entire unit knew what she was experiencing. Various versions would circulate, due to Mary unable to recollect the countless renditions of what was told. She probably thought the verbal disclaimer to every individual she disclosed testimony to-- that they were the sole beneficiary--would provide protection of her juicy tales remaining untold. WRONG!

Mary relishes being the center of attention around the male species. One Friday evening, she met some co-workers for a party at a nearby bar. As soon as I walked into work on Monday morning, I was approached with front page news details of what transpired: Mary had too much to drink, possessing the inability to drive herself home; throughout the evening she was dancing in a sexually suggestive manner on quite a few men, and one was even willing to take her home (it wasn't so they could bake brownies together). Her account on Monday morning: she desired to have fun and met an individual who removed her from the singles market. This "new found romance" lasted about a month, if that long. Soon to follow, a computer love.

Mary met 'RoShawn' on a free internet dating site. Within a week, she printed his profile picture to hang in her office as if he were her longtime boyfriend. In less than a month, she was gushing about how her children loved him (to the point of calling him daddy), and that the four of them felt like a genuine family. RoShawn was allowed to stay overnight at her residence beginning the first month of meeting. Due to our shared single parent status, I became concerned. My child does not meet every man that I go out with. Her opinion of me matters greatly, and I would never want her to consider mom as suggestively loose; dating large quantities of men as if they were in rotation. In addition, the profusion of pedophiles and sexual predators who would delight the opportunity to take advantage of our young ones, should be considered. Mary was unfazed when I expressed uneasiness. Dwelling selfishly in her own wants and desires, she stated how perfect he was for her. She allowed him full access into her home but was prohibited to enter his (he confessed embarrassment of his small apartment). Mary bought him clothes and accessories despite his lack of purchasing items for her. She financially fronted their trips while he promised reimbursement at a later date. OK...who's seeing red flags?

The affair was abolished by the end of the second month. Mary had discovered her fine fellow was a convicted felon, which he failed to confess. RoShawn wasn't even his first name! 'Troy RoShawn Jenkins' was the name listed on his birth certificate. If she would have entered it into the county court system, evidence of his arrest record would have been exposed. Mary announced the circumstances of how she found out, all the while searching for sympathy. We previously mentioned to initiate a background check and proceed slowly, but our warnings were ignored. Two weeks later, Mary exclaimed her engagement to a man she's known since childhood. We all shook our heads in disbelief, wondering why she was so desperate to be married.

Part of the foundation my parents set for me was to first, love myself; to find true contentment and comfort in my singleness. Being independent and secure allows me to proudly exude a high self-esteem; aware of my worth!

When one repeatedly searches for companionship, certain components prove to be lacking within the individual. Until the missing element(s) is identified and implemented, they will continue to ride the carousel of love.

Mary-Goes-Round

At the age of 38, Mary still goes around
In hopes of discovering a true love to be found
Her methods of unearthing this once in a lifetime chance
Always leads to destruction of a short-lived romance
Initially, so excited, she offers much of herself
Demands exclusivity—talking to no one else
Introductions of her child occur within just days
Satisfying her gentlemen in various ways
Purchasing clothes, trips and all they desire
To keep them around the stakes increase higher
Without thoroughly known she unhesitatingly trusts
And unveils her gift, which should be deemed most precious
When all's been dispersed and her account is dry
They depart the Mary-go-round to search another ride
Repeatedly, fault is on the gentleman's behalf
For their character was complicated, cunning and crass
Never does she divulge what we already know
That in order to have a man she'd sell her very soul
Mary feels significant and secure when on a man's arm
But her wretched relationships prove nothing but harm
The improper example provided for her child
The acceptance of the men who've done nothing but defile
Instead of seeking solace and strengthening herself
She's ready to commence, hunting for someone else
Happiness does not reside in the hands of a man
But from the Spirit that you hold within

If you have no love, first, for yourself
Guaranteed that so will no one else
Self-esteem and respect should be priority in life
To ensure you don't become a Mary-go-round ride

March 7, 2013

I had my first "official" boyfriend at the age of 19---'Ramsey'; a 24 year-old co-worker at a distribution center who was also a father of a two year-old son. We'd mostly see each other in passing. But one day while in the break room, we exchanged numbers and began talking on a frequent basis.

One evening, Ramsey asked me to come by for a visit. We were a couple of months into our relationship and I was excited when I pulled up to a house. It was an impressive accomplishment to be a homeowner at his age, I thought. Upon entering, I asked him why the lights weren't on since he greeted me with a hug in the dark. He stated he and his roommate had a rule: in order to save money on their electric bill, the lights remained off if neither were occupying the area (at 19 it sounds believable...as adults we're thinking yeah, right!). I'm instantly welcomed with pictures of his adorable son as I walked into his room. Ramsey spoke on being a father and inquired if I ever thought of having a family. My immediate response: yes, but not right now! I didn't want to give the impression I was ready to be someone's stepmother.

We sat close while watching television. Cuddling has the ability to rouse romantic thoughts and desires, which inevitably happened. I was apprehensive and scared, informing Ramsey that I was a virgin. His response was one of surprise.....however, he assured me he'd be gentle. My thoughts were fleeting a mile a second---should I or shouldn't I have sex with him? Although I wasn't in love, I did have feelings for him. Eventually, I consented. It was not the pleasurable experience my friends boasted it would be! When I yelled out in discomfort, Ramsey remarked, "Shhhh, quiet down—my parents are in the other room."

WHAT!!????!! (insert the sound of a record scratch) As soon as he made that known, I immediately flipped him over, told him to get up and get off, and dressed! Not only was I furious with him for lying about his "roommate", but also myself. I allowed this scrub to take a priceless gift that belonged to only ME! I branded him a loser and left. Ramsey tried to win me back with repetitious apologies. When I no longer accepted his calls, he wrote a note of intentions to reclaim the 24K gold chain he gave me. I had already sold it to a pawn shop

(I know that was mean, right?); receiving $40 for what I considered my troubles and his untruth. My first time was the worst time, which I could never recapture!

We know that Jesus paid the price for our sins with His life. Even though I sat in the church pews singing songs and halfway listening to sermons, I truly did not believe that I was worthy of forgiveness. I knew right from wrong and my parents had encouraged me to wait until my wedding night to save myself for my husband.

I prayed for God to listen to my sorrow, begged for forgiveness and promised I would never do it again (mmm-hmmm...we all know that promise wasn't kept). I was so turned off from sex and scared of becoming like a few of my friends; pregnant at a young age. I aspired to turn my life around and concentrate on things of great importance, which included my future.

All of us have made mistakes---whether lying, cheating, stealing, using others for personal gain, fornication, adultery, etc. God loves us so much that He is willing to forgive---but it's not a game! We're not to dive headfirst into sin on Monday through Friday, and then pray on Saturday night (mmm-hmm....trying to get right before Sunday morning church service); assuming that we're washed clean before our next premeditated, sinister offense!

When we fall on our knees we should plead for a sincere change--primarily with our thinking! The devil uses tempting power of suggestion with unfavorable things we meditate and dwell on. Ultimately, we make the choice! Win the battle in your mind....be strong and tame your thoughts, for they control your actions.

Even though we accept the fact that no one is perfect, we can live our lives striving to be that way, everyday! I thank God for the new mercies He gifts me every morning when I awake. Without Him, I would be nothing!

REGIFTED

I fell in love, at least that's what I thought
So young in age, so young at heart
Inexperienced as to how relationships should be
I gave my all and self completely

After my present was unwrapped
Suddenly problems began to happen
No-shows, arguments and constant fights
Led to our complete dissolve one night

Feeling used and hurt within
Lost at heart, consumed with sin
I knelt down on my knees to pray and meditate
To contemplate the choices I had made

I relinquished my body, pure and simple
Instead of treating it as the Lord's temple
Laying my soul down time after time
Hoping that his love I would find

While down in prayer my Lord spoke to me
And lovingly proclaimed that my sin was set free
Told me that there was no greater love
That an earthly man could give, compared to His above

As tears streamed down my face, Your mighty hand reached
To lift my head, caress and whisper unto me
"My love is more than enough for you to suffice
Your next relationship, make sure you go about right

T. Marie

Get to know the person for who they are
Their spirit and soul should shine like the brightest star
They should reverence Me and obey My commands
If done right, the two of you should withstand

You're as white as snow, your transgression is done
Be still as I drape clean garments back on
Just be patient for what I have in store..."

I've been re-gifted, made whole once more

February 23, 2009

Back in the day, I longed to become a professional singer. I deemed myself the next Janet Jackson: I could sing, dance, write songs and was told I had, "the look"! However, living in Ohio was not a prime location to reside if you wanted to launch a music career.....at least, when I was growing up.

Throughout the years, my feelings have changed regarding the music industry. Part of me is content that I chose not to fully pursue it. Who knows what kind of person I would have become.... I can only imagine. But with the way the entertainment business is now, you have to be nearly naked in order to get noticed. Forget the voice— crooning capabilities seem to matter not.

Take for instance, Mariah Carey...the woman can blow! When her career commenced with the hit song/video, 'Vision of Love', she was a fully clothed, innocent-looking, doe-eyed diva in the making. As the years progressed, despite singing ability, her chest endured a "miraculous metamorphosis"; multiplying in size. Her performance wardrobe consisted (and still does) of enticing attire—seemingly small for her frame. Mariah possesses a wondrous gift, however, half-dressed appearances distract from the angelic sounds she brings forth. What happened to the days of old; relying on the allure of the vocal instrument instead of ones physique?

Nowadays, Hollywood's walk toward fame can be easily accomplished via sex tapes. Thanks to Ray J (and his trusty video camera), Kim K was able to profit from her promiscuity. Due to her infamous intimacy, she boasts a fashion line, perfume, a television show, talk show appearances, movie rolls, etc. Her achievements caught the attention of a famous actor's daughter, who mentioned idolization of various celebrities who have traveled the path of publicized sexual trysts. She proclaimed her decision to enter the pornographic world while anticipating her rise to stardom........which still remains unfulfilled.

Include the abomination of drug and alcohol addictions, eating disorders and other harmful habits--- blatantly broadcast for all adoring fans to view. Actresses admit to starving themselves in order to don a designer dress for premiers and award presentations, which is beyond absurd! Think of the damaging effects to our emulative young people who are participating in overzealous acts, aiming towards becoming a carbon copy. The passion to obtain popularity by any means—partaking in illegal substances, fasting to fit the latest fashions and disobeying the law—can lead to a life of rehab (Lindsey Lohan), serving time in jail (Chris Brown), or an unfortunate, untimely death as River Phoenix and Amy Winehouse sustained.

We have our own children, literally dying----imitating what they perceive is a way to achieve greatness, money, adulation and notoriety. Celebrities should be celebrated for their craft, not heralded as if a modern-day messiah. They are just human beings holding a publicly displayed profession. Knowing this, their impressionable words and actions speak volumes, regardless of intentions.

It is our responsibility as parents, relatives, teachers, community leaders, etc., to favorably mold our future generations; leading and guiding them in the right direction. Instilling accountability, encouraging individuality and uplifting their self-esteem, will leave a positive, permanent imprint that influences the choices they make throughout their lives.

I thank God I'm content with my life and how I'm living it. Although I may not be able to afford luxurious automobiles or homes, I am rich in family, friends, and love!

UNHOLY-WOOD

My dreams of reaching national acclaim....
International fame, are trickling down the drain...
I don't possess the correct size of massive breasts and
narrow hips
My ribs don't stick out...my body and size proportionate
An unrecognizable individual, my family stock unknown
My daddy's not rich, I'm no heiress to a throne
I've never been to prison, my pants don't sag
Some might say at my age I'm just an old hag
I eat all of my food allowing it to digest
Not bringing it back up to fit the latest dress
I don't have chasing crowds demanding autographs
I know who my true friends are, confident I won't be stabbed
Preferential treatment unheard of, just like my name
I don't have 1 night stands, tape intimacies or play sex games
Objects and substances are disallowed in my nostrils
Or abundant alcoholic consumption to where I can no longer feel
I believe in and serve God—not illuminati or scientology
My confidence does not lie with others, for I believe in me
My picture won't auction off for the highest dollar
These surgery and sin-filled "role models" make me
wanna holla!!!
I'm not involved in scandals of who's doing who
I can't see myself paying $3000 for just a pair of shoes
I'm as laid back as they come and trustworthy to a T

T. Marie

If you want to approach, you're welcome to—there's no security
No paparazzi following and invading my privacy
I love my life of normalcy....
Just me, being me.......

June 27, 2007

Not long ago, I had a conversation with an African-American co-worker of mine. He stated that an inquiry came about my ethnicity: was I of a mixed heritage? Confused as to why a person would ask such a question, 'Darius' claimed that someone thought I was part Caucasian because of the music I listened to.

First of all, my genetic makeup should not provoke a concern for anyone that I work or share building space with. What the information would do for the curious is beyond me! Just like beauty being in the eye of the beholder, music stirs the ear and soul of the individual. We're allowed to play music at my place of employment, and when free from our assigned phone schedules, some of us turn on our radios or put ear buds in; allowing the sounds of relaxation to ease our stressful day. My repertoires of artists are vast: Color Me Badd, Kirk Franklin, Joss Stone, Steve Perry, Tye Tribbett, Luther Vandross, Billy Joel, and Keith Sweat (to name a few), along with numerous Motown artists. I set the volume just loud enough for my neighbor to hear and enjoy the free concert.

It was disappointing to hear the ignorant comments that Darius shared. I responded by blurting out, "Oh, so because I have brown skin on my body, everyone I listen to must look like me? I'm a musician, singer, and songwriter, but because I'm black I have to enjoy only "my kind" of music? That's one of the dumbest things I've ever heard!" Darius truly did not know what to say...... probably wishing he never approached me in the first place. In my opinion, whomever posed the question should have been immediately informed that my culture and musical preferences had no bearing on being an African-American.

Throughout my life, I've heard that my 'Black card' had expired, considering I care not to indulge in watermelon, animal tongues, cheeks, intestines, feet and behinds. Absolutely disgusting, is my belief! Enveloping the Black experience does not include ingesting of solely soul food, African-American authors, artists, designers, etc., for it limits ones growth and discovery of all the beautiful ethnic offerings and wonders of the world. It's pretty pathetic when your own race jests you're not "black enough", despite the lineage of your parents.

While growing up, my sister and I resided in a predominantly white neighborhood and attended the local schools. The few black students ridiculed her for sounding white. But I always wondered, how can you "sound like a color"? Was the problem because she didn't slur her words and speak slang, or that she spoke with an educated flair?

The world consists of various stereotypes of diverse cultures. Native Americans supposedly like to gamble and drink alcohol; Mexicans always live ten or more to a home; Asians are geniuses; Middle Easterns hate Americans (that perception heightened after 9/11) and Caucasians are rhythm-less nations (unable to dance) who are out to destroy all minorities. As for us African-Americans: we don't tip at restaurants, we're not intelligent, a large appetite for watermelon, fried chicken and Kool-Aid, the ability to run fast and play basketball, all of our Black men are well-endowed (Lord knows that's far from the truth!), we're drug lords, lazy, and our women have multiple children to retain welfare. Even though some of the statements are accurate for some individuals, it's unfair to group and deem those characteristics as factual for everyone. What needs to happen-- the discontinuation of ammunition for others to view us as worthless.

Case in point, saggin' pants. If there's one thing I can do without for the rest of my life, it's that ignorant "fashion statement"! People have claimed this trend originated in the prisons. Inmates who were willing to provide gratification would dangle their pants as a hint of availability. Supposedly, fans of the hip hop culture are supporting and mimicking their icons' clothing craze in order to appear cool and fashion forward. I'm displeased when I see people's pants drooping to their thighs; unable to walk with a normal stride.

To the embarrassment of my daughter, I stopped two young African-American men walking in front of us at a store with their underwear staring back at

56

us. *Calling out to them in a motherly tone, I asked why they felt the need to expose their drawers and sag their jeans. The answer I received, "I don't know, ma'am, I just like it." I explained that they were handsome gentlemen but the look took away from their personal display. I also discussed my dissatisfaction of my daughter and I viewing the undergarment that is supposed to be housed under their garments. They apologized....tucking and pulling everything together. I wonder if they truly realized how disheveled, unkempt and foolish they appeared, or if the young men even cared. Maybe if they spelled saggin' backwards, it might incite a change in their outward expression.*

Impressions are lasting. Seemingly, if one continuously views a culture performing a certain character or behaving in a particular manner, it's not unusual that the seed of stereotype has been planted. If we are to rebuild our credibility, we must take pride in who we are; instructing and motivating our people regarding the benefits of dreaming big! By increasing our awareness toward the negative misconceptions of us African-Americans, with a determined and united front, we can expunge the falsities that have so long kept us in bondage. Receiving a degree instead of a government check, excelling at studies rather than entirely on sports, and dignity in our presentation, promotes a promising future for all.

With perseverance, we can, and will, KEEP HOPE ALIVE!

COLOR CODED

Just because I'm forever tanned, you declare I must like rap
Wear my pants sagged and baggy with my hat to da' back
My picnic plate: watermelon, chitlins and the chicken fried
Collard greens, black-eyed peas with corn bread on the side
Walking with much swag and talkin' with the slang
My man needs to boast several tattoos, ears pierced with rings
In his ride, bass boomin'---tinted windows on the beamer
Expressions--- mean muggin' with a cool, ghetto-thug type demeanor
No hangin' at the library to get the brain stimulated
Teased for speaking white when I articulate educated
Only coffee in my circle, absent integration of cream
Is this what Dr. King meant when he said, "I have a Dream"?
Our children are listening to gangsta music, lyrics memorized
Without the successful ability to add, subtract, multiply and divide
We're loitering at the corner store to rob for the next meal
Practicing private medicinal transactions, otherwise known as drug deals
Babies are having babies, kids are killing kids
Such an unacceptable way for our people to live
Ancestors fought desperately and died for rights of equality
But with the seeds we're presently sowing, our harvest still remains weak
Granted, we have a President who resembles someone like me
Is this example enough to inspire us all with desire to achieve?
We're more than just a basketball, a football or some random sport
Without passion to receive a degree, we're selling ourselves short
The world has plenty of entertainers entertaining on the stage
We're in dire need of professionals to impact our world today

An astronaut, scientist, or college professor is attainable if you believe
For we all possess characteristics for the betterment of society
Accepting mediocrity is unsatisfactory if pursuing to raise the bar
Performing proactively to advance and elevate will take you far
Although so many of us have not produced to our fullest potential
Reciting affirmations and generating goals prove to be essential
Conforming to cultural stereotypes will result a life of less
Than what God intended for all His children-- nothing short of success
Having sat on the sidelines long enough, it's time to enter the game
Don't allow opportunities to pass you by...It's never too late for change!

December 7, 2013

T. Marie

Every Sunday evening I feel the pangs of mental stress and anguish. I reflect on the fact that for the following five days, I am required to show up for work and remain in an environment that I deem, at times, repugnant!

All throughout the week my job commands my presence on the phones. I cannot begin to tell you how many ignorant, prejudice and thoughtless individuals I speak to. People want problems solved when they have the ability to initiate the task on their own. In addition to daily customer service, I am responsible for precise determinations on various claims. If the claimant performed an erroneous action or pertinent information is pending, the process can be extremely time consuming. Oh—I forgot to mention…we're short staffed!

To sum it all up, supervisors who feel they are God's gift prance about the department. Two of them have been allowed to turn the place into a nightmare with their carelessness, incompetence, and downright disrespectful attitudes! They possess schizophrenic and bi-polar tendencies; one moment they're lying about you and ten minutes later, with a "polite" disposition, ask how your day is going. Confusion and disorder have completely soiled our unit without anyone attempting to thoroughly clean it up.

Granted, I thank God every day for my job! It is a blessing to have the financial means to support myself and my daughter. However, I long to have employment elsewhere. Namely, becoming my own boss!

To own and have full control of a company is my heart's desire! I'd choose who I want to employ and work with, and which insurance company I desire benefits from instead of the employer's selection being forced upon me. Best of all, I'd awaken every day with a smile on my face---- basking in the realization of achieving and living my dream!

Even though I have yet to fulfill my destiny, I am decisively disciplined; climbing every mountain until I victoriously ascend to the highest peak! Never negative, never letting go, and never giving up!

Until then, it's time to make the doughnuts!

WAKE UP CALL!!!!!

6AM- I'm summoned from the sounds
Squawking screams of alarm
Informing that my day is to begin
However, I desire my start to stop
To prevent the pending madness
Daily dysfunction endured over forty hours a week
Pompous persons that behold titles
That would never grant entrance into Heaven
Bigoted behavior, due to the caramelization of my skin
Set-up stings, meant to entrap those in their vicinity
To rid those deemed unwelcome, unwanted, and unwilling to play the game
This playa chooses not to participate in foolish folly
With undeserving opponents
But to play the game of life, with my life
The one life God granted me to make the most of
Which does not consist of confining cubicles
Completely free to pursue my promise, my purpose
Sooner, rather than later
Refusing to allow myself to miss my moment
This is the era I claim my calling
To shine, to beam, to glimmer, to gleam
It's time to shake up the wake up
Because the tick-tock of time halts for no one
So, for all you spectators out there
Get ready, get set.....

WATCH FOR ME!!!!!!

June 16, 2013

T. Marie

Each and every day of my work week is busy! I cram in 8.5 hours of employment, exercise, homework, dinner duties, and additional appointments on a required basis. My Friday evenings consist of dates with household chores instead of dinner and a movie....enabling the ability of having a less laborious weekend. Saturdays are designated for completing my work detail. But I do have one rule I aim to observe: SLEEPING IN!

My family is aware of the terms I've established prior to 10:00 am---do not ring my bell---whether the front door or through the wires! Nevertheless, my mom recently breached the verbal contract before my daily regimen was activated. Dueling with indecision, I answered the call; aggravated with myself for not turning the phone off the previous night. After the implementation of my appointed restriction, the request had been honored. Although I was too tired to contemplate, a genuine reason had to warrant her summoning.

On Friday evening, mommy expressed discomfort in her shoulder area. It swelled overnight; radiating extreme pain within the region by the following morning. On Sunday she was responsible for providing a vegetable tray at her church's reception, and asked if I'd go to the store and purchase the items. Mommy knows she can rely on me to assist when in need, however, despite my undying love for her, I wrestled with thoughts of surfacing from my slumber. A touch perturbed after a ten minute conversation, I hurriedly dressed in anticipation of an effortless task.

Finding the vegetables was an easy undertaking but the dip was my downfall! With every unsuccessful search for a specific flavor, I groaned and grumbled when entering and exiting multiple stores empty-handed! Hearing my complaints of inconsideration, I took a moment to LISTEN to my vocals. What nerve—to whimper and whine while portraying the role of mom's personal assistant! Throughout my life of ups and downs, not once has she ever hesitated to help me--always readily willing and available--even at a moment's notice. I was behaving selfishly, for the sleep I was currently sacrificing could be acquired by way of an afternoon nap. Putting my priorities in order, I was able to complete her shopping list and deliver the goods. I was richly rewarded with a thank you, a hug and a loving smile of appreciation!

There are a few individuals I know who would eagerly accept the opportunity to be at their parent's beck and call. They are left with only pictures and memories of their loved ones. I'm blessed with the pleasure to see, speak, kiss, hear and touch mine on a regular basis. But, the mistake a lot of us make is taking time and each other for granted. We are all traveling this journey called life and every journey, unfortunately, has an end.

Regardless of my busy, individual household, never does a day pass without my family hearing and knowing how much I love them. So take advantage of one another's presence. You never know when the gift of life will be returned to its rightful owner!

ONCE MORE

Remembering the song you used to sing
The aggravating anthem, Monday through Friday mornings
Announcing preparation of our school day routine
Prying probes pertaining to daily activities
As a detective investigating the crime of the century
Enslaved to perform weekly household chores
For a meager 20 cent allowance of satisfaction
Snores that signaled all the barnyard animals home
Earsplitting orchestras requiring responses of 'God Bless You'
The echoes of enjoyment while nibbling nourishment
Resembled the slosh of slop at a piglet's potluck
The gaseous fumes exhaled from your being
Poisonously potent to generate a nuclear power plant
The dissection of nerves with repetitious requests
Repeatedly fazed me....But I'm missing you like crazy!!!

Now that you've traveled to reside at your Father's house
Abandoned from all your five senses
No longer able to hear vivacious laughter
Or view the grace you beheld as you sat on your throne
Your encompassing caresses unable to protect me
Absent the aroma of your lingering fragrance
Home cooked meals are permanently past
I'd pay any price for unceasing solicitations
Belches deemed beautiful, this time around
Excessive explorations, an enthusiastic event

Salivating smacks, a glorious sound
How I wish for the opportunity to appreciate your entirety
A day...An hour....A second
Just to have you here with me........

Once again..............

February 15, 2014

Being pregnant with my daughter is, and always will be, one of the most ecstatic and fulfilling events of my lifetime! I've always wanted children, and at one point thought about adopting if I hadn't married by the age of thirty (I married at the age of twenty-nine). Regardless, I thank God I was blessed to naturally experience the journey of pregnancy.

Everything was so new to me—the various changes occurring within; a swollen stomach and painful breasts to hot flashes, burps and gas that would've blown up the entire block! Unexplained crying spells and mood swings were accompanied with cravings for salad and french fries. Now, all of these symptoms do not sound the least bit attractive or comfortable, but nothing could compare to the bonding of this mother and her child!

I talked to my temporary tenant on a daily basis. I caressed my ever-expanding belly as if she were in my arms that very moment. I told 'Pookie-woo' about my world, what I longed her world to become and the plans I had for us. I imagined her physical features and put in a request to God....Please, let her be healthy!!

I became overly-anxious for her arrival as the days, weeks, and months passed by! During my last exam, excitement peaked when my OBGYN informed me that I was 3cm dilated. I could either go to the hospital and walk the halls to promote further dilation or return home to do the same. Choosing the latter, I called my friends and family to prepare them for Jalyn's birth!

There was a point and time during labor that I sustained a slight scare. The doctor stated Jalyn's head was stuck and to cease pushing. Worry engulfed me as various thoughts crossed my mind: 'Can she still breathe? Is she going to be alright? Do I need to undergo a C-section?' A couple of minutes later, which seemed like an eternity, I was told to resume pushing. Soon thereafter, I was rewarded with a beautiful, screaming baby girl!

I reached out for her but a nurse intercepted in order to clean and wrap her up. When I felt she was taking too long, I demanded my child in a way a mother- "out of labor-I did all this work by myself-carried her for nine months and I'm tired- so you better c'mon!!!"-could voice.

As my mini-me was placed in my arms, I cried. Viewing this priceless, perfect and precious life that God entrusted me to raise, teach and love for the rest of my years, moved me tremendously! I could not comprehend unconditional love until I had my daughter.

She is, forever, My Precious!

My Precious

From the first time I knew you were within
You captured my heart like no other
Sensations of our bodies intertwined as one
Became the most amazing wonder of my world
Dependent as rain to a flower
Love blossomed inside my heart, my soul
Distractions ceased, Intrusions ignored
My focus fixated on you
My Precious......
As months went by, your radiant sun
Showered me with a glorious glow
Anxiously awaiting your impending arrival
Imagining birthing a new beginning
You left the warmth of your home
And leapt into the warmth of my arms
The most beautiful sight overwhelmed my entire being
As endless emotions and triumphant cries
Joyously filled the air
You are my love, Forever my daughter....
My Precious....

November 9, 2006

As far back as I can remember, there's always been an issue regarding the various shades within the African-American race. Origination began when slave owners raped their female property----breeding a generation of mulatto, or mixed-race children. Possessing lighter skin and a fine texture of hair, no longer did they resemble the traditional, more African looking slave. During maturation, privileges were bestowed. Executing daily responsibilities in the Big House, such as cooking, caring for the white children, or meeting their Master's/Misses' "personal needs", were positions that provided better working conditions. Even though the employees were still deemed slaves, not having to perform hard labor in the fields was considered an advantage. It's safe to assume that the distinct separation of pigmentation generated jealousy; creating ample animosity within the Black community.

In the 1920's (era of the Cotton Clubs), segregation of African-Americans persisted. Although establishments showcased prominent white celebrity entertainment, most of the acts and staff were people of color. However, the chorus girls had a prerequisite of standing at least, 5'6" tall, light-skinned (with a minimal hue) and under the age of 21. Being a woman with an unilluminated appearance was unacceptable.

Black American societies, fraternities, churches and civic groups, prolonged the prejudice with their own provisions; one being, the brown paper bag test. If you were darker in comparison to a brown paper bag, exclusion was the clinching consequence. Blue Vein Societies (light enough to visibly see the veins bluish-hue on your forearms) also represented the upper and upper-middle classes. Sponsoring balls as meeting places for eligible, identical counterparts, enabled the division of dignitaries from those deemed disgraceful.

In this present day, we continue to carry the torch of torturing one another over the very same issue that angers us when demonstrated by other ethnicities. On February 24, 2012, in St. Louis, MO, 'The Venue' held a contest called, Battle of the Complexions. The nightclub's competition promised an answer to the inquiry---What's the sexiest skin complexion? Not only did the challenge devalue the female participants, progression to promote disharmony and disintegration pressed on.

Before Plymouth Rock landed on us, as Malcolm X once declared, our African ancestors were one of unity; a family that cared for one another. Due to the seeds Europeans sowed within us, a harvest of hatred infiltrated our people from the days of old. During the Civil Rights movement, Dr. Martin Luther King preached and sang, "We shall overcome, someday". How is that achievable if we're still seizing slave mentalities? Man does not dictate what is appealing and attractive, for beauty is in the eye of the beholder. Whether a cafe' latte, caramel or deep mocha flavor, every individual is a spectacular creation designed by God!

Once African-Americans are able to love and accept themselves and each other, will we truly be Free At Last!

2 SHADES OF LOVE

I once thought preconceived opinions only existed on the outside
Discrimination, due to the ownership of a certain color scheme
Never imagined my kin would shun and imprison
My worthiness, based on the skin I live in
I'm the elephant in the room...seen, yet invisible
Acknowledgment of my presence is on a sliding scale
I'm the Cinderella that never arrived at the ball
The slave, out in the field, undeserving of Master's house
*While the luminescent **LIGHT** glistens for all to see*
*My **DARK**ness deafens and blinds those surrounding me*
Regardless of my comprehensible spoken words
Translation is in the form of a foreign language
Accomplishments are many, however, somewhat unmemorable
Compared to those of my golden opponent
Her accolades are sung by angelic choruses
Handwritten in the history books for generations to come
A pristine pathway leading to a perfected life
My obstacle-filled odyssey has left me wandering...
Wondering...
Is not the bond of blood that runs through our veins
Undeniably Binding?
My possession of multiplied melanin
Negates not my position within a biased bloodline
Although the innocent adolescent
Immaturity and ignorance grace the wise elders
Continuation of pastime prejudices
As if presently picking cotton under the Southern sun
My hue cannot hide my humanness
Or the longing for love and equality

T. Marie

Pigmentation, whether a Lovely light
Beautiful brown or Desirable dark
Unchanges the truth
That all Black blood bleeds red

November 29, 2013

When engaged in a relationship, it's fascinating how others have an acute awareness or assessment of the person we're involved with. Are we so captivated and immersed that we tend not to recognize particular warning signs of an individual, or does our personal agenda dim the discernment we once depended on? There are numerous grounds as to why we look the other way and endure certain behaviors, situations and circumstances.

When heading towards my late twenties, I recall pending thoughts of marriage--wondering if a trip down the aisle was in my future. Although I wasn't the type of woman to date just "anything", I had my share of relationships. I was on the finicky side but not excessively choosy (my parents would probably disagree). I do understand and realize that no one is perfect. Nevertheless, I desired a marriage comparable to one my parents possess; a beautiful, everlasting love affair between the best of friends. I sought to find a man closely resembling the characteristics of my dad: a God-fearing, sacrificial, hard-working man who loves his family.

I happened to meet 'Jody'; a member of my church and choir. He seemed like a nice person, had a decent singing voice and a nice smile. During a conversation, he informed me that he worked two jobs and proudly stated that his mom said he was her favorite child (he has additional siblings), which I deemed a close relationship. We dated, met each others' families, and spent quite a bit of time together in and outside of church. One evening he came over to my house, and somehow we ended up in an argument over refrigerated bottled water. I had previously asked him to keep his unfinished ones on one side while mine remained on the opposite. Accidentally placing his incorrectly, which was not an astronomical issue for me, I reminded him of the arrangement. He immediately raised his voice....spewing sarcastic comments! I looked at him with wonder. Who was this person ranting about the most simplistic request? At the time of the incident we were involved in premarital counseling sessions at church. I mentioned the quarrel to the Pastor, but was encouraged to believe that it could be the devil trying to sever our relationship (it could have been God revealing this was not the man for me). Jody apologized and I shelved the episode. We never experienced another dispute throughout the remainder of our dating relationship (our marriage was the exact opposite).

An additional red flag came from his mother. Some of my church friends held a bridal shower for me at a restaurant. Jody's mom and sisters were in attendance and everyone brought gifts to celebrate my impending nuptials the following weekend. I received skimpy nighties, lotions, perfumes, and a weekend getaway for our honeymoon! However, his mother's contribution vanquished my entertaining and enjoyable evening. Her offering was a book; nothing informative regarding intimacy and marriage, or concerning romantic trips for two. No--the title of this book was, 'How to Encourage Your Mate's Self-Esteem'--as if his were low or non-existent! I stared at the book, wondering if I should allow the women around the table to view it as I had done with every prior present. Slightly embarrassed and not wanting others to view my fiancee' as a tentative loser, I held the book up for half of a second while internally questioning the intent.

For the remainder of the evening, my thoughts were fixated on the title of the book. If Jody's mother knew he had issues, why would she not verbally disclose and discuss them with me? I felt she had an obligation but she might have considered her contribution sufficient enough for me to have second thoughts. I consulted my mom, and even though she regarded it quite different to bestow such an offering to a forthcoming daughter-in-law, it didn't necessarily signify a spirit-less self-esteem.

Looking back, I probably should have postponed the wedding. Allowing more time would've enabled me to delve under additional, negative layers that surfaced after we married. Were there signs? Yes, but I temporarily casted potential predicaments aside, which eventually dissolved our marriage.

Regardless of other people's perceptions and opinions, take heed to your own instincts, conscience, and premonitions. View realistically, not through rose-colored glasses. It could preserve you from inevitable, life-altering disasters.

Pre-Marital Premonition

On Valentine's Day you dropped to one knee
And professed your sincere and undying love for me
Til the last of your breaths you wanted to spend
Together, conjoined, until our eternal end
How I've longed this moment to become reality
But we've been dating nine months—more remains to be seen
On the surface you seem to be the perfect guy
But beneath, reality reveals specks in my eyes
Insistent, you can be, when I don't sway your way
There've been instances to where you held grudges for days
Opinionated is fine if you had an open stance
But you can be tightly closed to where no one stands a chance
To those in need you volunteer your time
But when I come up short, from me, you hide
Majestic, grand entrances are your pleasure
While my modest and humble don't quite measure
You were born to be wild and live so free
Which is probably what initially attracted me
I'm wondering if our relationship is somehow unstable
We should confront these issues I see on the table
You mentioned how my virtue could transform you
But the choice to change is solely yours to do
The more I contemplate, while you're on bended knee
Just to become a bride. I can't commit willingly
I desire to be married but standards must be met
Time needs to be allowed to pray and reflect

T. Marie

At this moment a union, seriously, would go awry
A review of my checklist is required to recognize if you're the guy
So I must decline your proposal for there's much I foresee
And I refuse to embark a disastrous matrimony

February 15, 2013

The process of dating is not what it used to be. Friends and family would introduce their closest and loved ones to people they knew, students would meet in high school or college, and co-workers "worked" on a more intimate level after hours (remember my motto--Don't have a honey where you make your money!).

Internet dating is extremely popular nowadays, and not entirely looked upon as being an act of desperation. Individuals with demanding jobs and careers can enjoy the flexibility it provides; searching for someone to spend time with despite having the freedom to explore. For those who are unappreciative of the blind date, including graduates from the club/bar environment thirsting for a new outlet, corresponding with other subscribers supplies the opportunity to weigh compatibility prior to meeting.

I tried internet dating for awhile, which produced a few relationships. One happened to be out of state, posing the question: who is willing to move? With my family base beside me, that was out of the question. He enjoyed his job and locality, reluctant in pursuing relocation. Moving is a huge sacrifice for one to make when your future together is uncertain, but the more I discovered about 'Grant', our relationship would have failed.

'Scott', the first Caucasian man I ever dated, resided an hour away from me. Although living in the same state, we spoke for about three months prior to meeting. I was pleased to see that he was true to his profile; conversationally as well as physically. However, a variety of nuisances were uncovered and our parenting styles were on the opposite ends of the spectrum.

Even though the relationships did not last, I had the chance to test the waters from a distance—delving deeper into both men on a personal level without the physical elements. I was privileged to encounter two very nice gentlemen, but there are some less fortunate than myself. Isolated individuals longing for love have fallen victim to profile predators. Due to written expressions of what one is seeking, ravenous receivers on the other side of the computer will dissect and calculate the vulnerability of their potential prey.

While viewing a talk show one afternoon, the host interviewed a woman in the midst of an online relationship. 'Samantha' had been communicating with 'Robert' for some time without the two ever having met. Robert's profile picture presented him as a Caucasian man, although his voice sounded like a Black African man (Samantha was shown conversing with him over a speaker phone). The distinct quality of his tone, amid the accent, puzzled the audience as to why she believed the image he featured. Over a year had surpassed without him unveiling his true, physical appearance in person, but Samantha stated she had fallen in love with Robert. Having planned numerous rendezvous, impromptu excuses always canceled their upcoming engagements; allowing him to cash in the unused plane tickets she purchased.

Robert played with her emotions; petitioning money to assist with various charity causes, his personal finances, settling of accounts and obligations, alongside the promise of a new beginning once he moved in with her. His verbal vows were vacant, but Samantha pursued and pressed forward with the relationship. Her friends and family expressed great concern that she was being taken advantage of, despite her claims that Robert truly loved her.

The host of the show displayed a list of every financial withdrawal she made for her distant companion. She cashed in her 401K and children's life insurance policies (which they discovered on the show), sold heirlooms and antiques, along with other numerous items. Altogether, she furnished over $400,000 of her funds to a masked man she professed passion for, in spite of the inability to identify face-to-face.

Anyone can cunningly conceptualize a scam to take advantage of others when involving internet relationships. A dating profile is predominantly the blueprint that is needed to initiate the strategy. When an individual reveals a strong desire to marry or a lengthy period of time since their last date, that pertinent information can ignite a layout of lies; forming a diabolical design to entrap their target. Unfortunately, we live in a world where people fabricate fairy tales to feed their self-gratifying ways.

When embarking on a new relationship, regardless of where you meet, have general conversations that omit personal and emotional elements. Always perform a background check (a ritual I practice) to ensure the person you're involved with is of good measure and standing. Use your file cabinet upstairs (mental notes are priceless), including intuition. Don't allow your conscious and compassion to duel! God blessed us with a spirit of discernment; advising us about the choices we ultimately make. When you lead with your head instead of your heart, falling victim to the wiles of a wolf in sheep's clothing can be avoided.

WEB OF LIES

Your profile of a lonesome life, for some time
Encourages and motivates my creative and devious mind
With a few keystrokes I concoct a strategy
Tempting and teasing your copious curiosity
Fabricating falsehoods to keep our dialogue alive
I disclose a make and model of luxury I drive
The degrees I don't have, rental properties I don't possess
My sympathetic, simulated secrets I gradually confess
While your heartstrings are pulled at a slow yet steady pace
Photographs are presented of muscularity and chiseled face
Your emotions exposed, revealing feelings within
Proceeding with my plan as an old-fashioned gentleman
To create a closer bond there's no other choice
Than exchanging phone numbers to sense the sound of your voice
Roses and candy sent to your place of business
Plagiarized poetry narrated to impress
Continuing conversation extracting information I need
Confessing, with you, is where I sincerely want to be
Although distance is the enemy in our computer romance
You'd give up everything to be together, if given the chance
Unable to uproot and relocate all you've accomplished
I offer to dismantle, proving to be unselfish
However, my monetary is tied up in investments
In order to proceed I'd require financial assistance
I find it quite odd......we've never formally met
Ready to withdraw funds as if deeply desperate
Twenty thousand dollars would ease my transition
As I sell my home and resign from my position
After affairs are liquidated and five figure payout received

We'll establish a beautiful union- just you and me
Extraction from your employer's 401K
Anticipating an effortless and extensive payday
Rapidly rushed via overnight express
Deposited to an untraceable P.O. Box address
A faux driver's license used to obtain
Proved to be a successful scheme, once again
The bond we had built was mortared with words
That you began trusting as soon as they were heard
A background check you never did pursue
Just an overwhelming desire for someone to love you
A hefty price was paid for this love affair
When charged to acquire affection, buyer beware
Always investigate to authenticate if their truths are a lie
For you're unaware who you'll encounter on the other side

December 15, 2013

I wasn't the most stunning young lady growing up, but I sho' nuff wasn't ugly (say that in your best Shug Avery voice)! I had my very first boyfriend as a sophomore in high school. 'Terance' dumped me after our two week courtship because I wouldn't permit him to peek and retrieve some change from my "pocketbook" (ladies, you know exactly what I'm talking about). Even though his actions were disappointing, I was neither depressed nor disturbed being discarded (he has four children by four different women, so I'm good). What's between my legs did not (and does not) define me. I regarded myself as a feminine tomboy and athlete; focused on enhancing my skills and homework.

It didn't take long to realize that the young ladies who permitted brazen physical contact or boasted their baby bump were consenting the contents in their purses. I was raised to abstain and have sex until I became a married woman (ooops...I guess by now you've realized I didn't quite make it). My parents stressed the fact that inner beauty--your character, personality, morals and values--are what counts the most. The exterior of a person can be deemed exquisite, but might be considered unattractive if accompanied with an appalling attitude.

I was blessed to reside in a household where old school principles--taking exceptional care of your self, spouse, and working together--provided a template of the various traits an individual, as well as a couple, should own. My mom taught me how to cook and clean, which society affirms a woman's duties. I observed her tenacity, strength and the ability to multi-task successfully. My dad instilled a firm work ethic, financial maturity and responsibility. He educated on the benefits of eating well and exercise, which continues to be important components of my daily regimen. Independence was crucial; the capability to do for myself, such as changing car tires and maintaining the maintenance of my vehicle.

We all know you should not judge a book by its cover. The pages need to be thoroughly read before one can make a concise conclusion as to whether it's a worthy read or needs to be shelved. The compilation of qualities and characteristics that cemented my foundation created me into the woman I am: a bit complex, somewhat stubborn, but passionate and powerful--- exceedingly and abundantly more than what meets the eye!

If you only knew.......

If you only knew what was before you.....

The gift of life in this 5'5" frame
The necessities that you need for daily survival
Wants and desires that you thought
Existed only in your dreams...
But could be fulfilled at the sound of your tenor articulation
I'm not speaking on just the physical....
But the entire realm....
Mental, Emotional and Spiritual stimulation
A smile that eclipses the light of the sun
A touch that soothes your injured and tender soul
The strength of a lioness, the purr of a kitten...
A domestic Goddess, Queen of the Castle
Reigning beside you, with you..
Together
An eternal and faithful sponsor of all your endeavors...
A caterer of nourishment and sustenance
In every capacity
Your soul will overflow with laughter and joy...
Insatiable passion will overtake you
As you're helplessly subject to my prowess
All of this...
Consists...
Embodied within this 5'5" frame

And now that you know............?

March 12, 2008

After one of my daughter's volleyball games I was introduced to 'Antonio'. A fellow parent informed me that his wife's ex-brother-in-law was interested in meeting me. He expressed how nice of a guy he was, so I agreed. We spoke after the game and throughout our 15 minute conversation discovered common interests, as well as mutual acquaintances. We exchanged phone numbers; gradually talking and texting on a daily basis. Within a couple of months, he'd visit about every other weekend when my daughter was with her father. Although we felt extremely comfortable with each other, I had no idea that the route we were traveling would take a turn for the worse.

My sister's employer was having a Christmas party she wanted me to accompany her to. This evening was to be an after five affair; the type of event I hadn't attended in awhile, which overwhelmed me with excitement! Antonio happened to drop by my house that Saturday afternoon, so I showed him the outfit I was going to wear. He pleaded for a picture of me with the classy, beige dress on. I agreed I would take one and stop by his house after the festivities.

The party was fabulous! The venue was located at a lavish hotel, we savored a deliciously catered meal, and the entertainment ranged from Christmas trivia to getting your groove on the dance floor. I checked my cell phone an hour into the celebration. My daughter called, which I returned and Antonio had text me. He hoped I was having a great time, mentioning that he hadn't yet received a picture. I replied of my enjoyment and would send one soon. His next statement surprised me.... requesting that I send a picture of me AND my sister. It seemed odd. I didn't immediately address my perception of his petition (he wanted proof that I was with her), but later took our picture and sent one to his and my niece's phone. His response: we looked beautiful.

I went to visit Antonio after the function ended. I didn't plan on staying too long for I had danced quite a bit and felt slightly sweaty. Not only that, I consumed a glass of wine (I hadn't indulged alcohol in over eight years) and was tired... it was almost midnight. The main purpose for the visit---for him to see me in my dress and view his residence for the first time.

I stayed about 30 minutes. We talked and watched television for a bit, however, I was ready to leave, go home, shower and get some sleep. He made a slightly sarcastic comment on how I had just arrived. Nevertheless, I stood up and put my coat on. When asked if he was ready to walk me to the door, he retrieved the remote to change the channels. With my patience dwindling, I walked down the hall, turned into his walk-in kitchen area and came around on the other side, inquiring, "Are you going to walk me to the door?" Antonio blankly glanced at me without responding. "Goodbye!" I said, and abruptly left. I could not believe his rude and discourteous behavior! It's after midnight and I'm walking myself to my own car! I was already driving down the street by the time he called. Not wanting to speak to him at that time, I refused to answer.

Having received numerous texts and voice messages apologizing for his conduct, I finally decided to speak to him two days later. I relayed that not escorting me to my car was a completely selfish and childish act. I also embarked on the subject of him wanting a picture of myself and my sister. I felt he had trust issues from happenings in some of his past relationships, which he said occurred almost 20 years ago! It's as if the picture validated her presence. He stated since he'd previously met her, he wanted a picture of us both. Even though I personally knew his brother, I assured Antonio that I'd only want a picture of him, being he's my man.

The conversation continued with inexhaustible drama; an emotion I do not embrace. The numerous attempts of clarifying behaviors and details was too much for me. When I announced we should decelerate, he responded defensively. I asserted that the recent argument had resulted in my resolution to ease up on our relationship. We'd still communicate but on a less frequent basis. I needed time to reveal if our association would advance.

We never recovered after my demands to downsize our schedule. Antonio was laid off from his job when we met, which was alright with me (he's a union worker); I understand that his occupation potentially provides inconsistent employment. However, he wanted to spend his abundance of free time with me, while I'm a single mother handling my ample responsibilities. I realized with the trust issues he possessed, my absenteeism could heighten his uncertainty to the point of conjuring an incessant curiosity.

Insecurity is one of the worst traits one can embody and I refuse to compromise my duties, dreams, goals and time, in order to secure a person's paranoia.

THE AIR I BREATHE

The air I breathe does not consist
Of your polyester fabrics or cotton blends
No jersey material do I constantly want to see
Or feel silk boxers sliding underneath me
Tube socks are faux pas on the rod of my shower
And the haze of aftershave leaves my stomach turning sour
The breath from your morning is not the perfect greeting
Along with constant shadowing, which proves you extremely needy
Your schedule seems to amount to countless hours of play
While single motherhood, homework and employment weigh down my 18hr days
Right now, not much going on for you but that has got to change
Because the once bright skies that shone are turning to a downpour of rain
Everywhere I need to be, you want to be right there
If this is your idea of love than I wish you no longer cared
Single—yes, that I am, and still intend to be
But I'm suffocating because you are the air asphyxiating me
Adorable it is to check on me throughout the day
Though ceaseless and unyielding calls are truly not the way
The repetitive, careless whispers make me want to holler out loud
I haven't proclaimed vows to God—dating is what we're about
How can I breathe without air of my own—I still aspire to be free
To continue being the individual I was before you ever met me
You need to back off, back up, and back out, so I can move around
And try to comprehend the reason I have to sit you down

I need no manager, supervisor, monitor, or even a chaperone
Productive I was before when I was truly on my own

Contamination free is how I live to breathe
A life of peace, tranquility and flawless purity

December 20, 2012

T. Marie

This poem was inspired by one of my previous co-workers, 'Marie'. She was married with children, and we became close acquaintances after being introduced by a mutual friend. Marie was an extremely trendy and stylish dresser who spent quite a bit of time, money and care into her appearance. Her walk contained a switch so hard that with every step the ground would tremor (OK- maybe I'm exaggerating a bit). She possessed a giving nature, but always desired kudos for her charity.

Speaking of charity, our employer held an annual fundraiser that emulated the show, 'American Idol'. In 2005 we both competed (along with two other individuals); representing our unit in hopes of moving forward to the next round. We performed our talent and the audience members would buy a vote for their favorite act by placing dollars in our assigned money jar.

When the competition was over, we assisted in carrying the supplies back to the event coordinator's office so she could count the money. But before she could begin, Marie wrote herself a check for fifty dollars and placed it in her jar; not with sincere intentions but in the hopes of winning the contest by any means necessary!

Later on that afternoon, 'Tabitha' emailed the results and announced Marie as the winner. She personally informed me it was a close race between us both, but she won by a slim margin with her last minute offering. Even though Marie's antics were a turnoff, I still expressed the wonderful time I had performing.

Word infiltrated all four floors of our office building as to how Marie "honestly" won. Fellow employees were in disbelief as to the measures she executed to be proclaimed the winner. She unveiled her lack of self-esteem and self-image through her actions, as peers now viewed her in a different light. By her outward appearance, they presumed that she was poised and confident. They presumed wrong.

Too many of us fraudulently front and fake our way through life just to look good for others. Enticing attention should not be a focal point to where one implements desperate tactics for a spotlight. Authenticity trumps imitation! When the love you have for yourself radiates, others will be drawn to the GENUINE you!

90

The Illusionist

All these women, here at work, surrounded by my presence
As I fabulously stride by they all inhale my intoxicating essence
The switch in my walk makes men dizzy with utter pleasure
While the girls dream jealously to be like me, by any measure
I can't blame them...after all, a total package, that I am
My coattail's extremely heavy due to all my adoring fans
Complimented everyday on any and everything
I've even been told that when I speak it sounds as if I sing
My clothes, fashionable, up to date in the latest styles
If a blind man turned in my direction I would surely make him smile
My voluminous hair blows in the breeze, like the mane of a Clydesdale
While the ladies sport jacked-up weaves bought from a clearance sale
Teeth so white it would make opaque pearls green with envy
My perfected porcelain skin......fine and smooth, tastes so creamy
Two graduate degrees from Harvard make me a rare commodity
Although I'm not bragging, just wondering, who wouldn't want to be me?
Could it be the woman whose unemployed husband dotes on her night and day?
While I can barely keep a working man three months before they stray
Or maybe it's the single mom who has two rambunctious children?
While various sexual diseases have already left my womb barren
What about that sista who drives a two-toned, low budget ride?
While I own a Lexus, even though it breaks down all the time
Possibly the lady who can only afford a one-bedroom home
While I have a plush, spacious penthouse, for which I took out a hefty loan

T. Marie

People always seem to think I got it going on
But if they looked much deeper, they'd conclude themselves to be wrong
For what you see before you sometimes is not what seems to be
But it's alright—for I'll continue to sway and portray
The illusion that perceives me.....

April 16, 2007

When it comes to raising children we know, for the most part, blood, sweat and tears will be involved!

My moody and sarcastic teenage daughter thinks she knows everything, despite the fact that she has lived on God's green earth for a mere fifteen years! Her growing pains and hormones resemble a trek to the highest cliff; the climb can be mighty rough, slips and falls may occur, but you feel a sense of accomplishment and satisfaction once you've reached the top. There are times when you feel like taking a much needed break from the mental stress, physical pangs and overall exhaustion! A rest is necessary in order to replenish what you've lost, recharge your battery and resume your expedition.

My precious girl has a medical condition: Neurofibroma Type I, where tumors can grow internally and/or externally, along with a brain tumor. I thank God her tumors are non-cancerous! Continuously experiencing pain in her right abdomen area, she had been prescribed a couple of medications in order to ease the discomfort. Now, I'm the type of mom who does her research prior to taking prescriptions, but for whatever reason I didn't this time around....maybe I just forgot. Let me just say, I wish I would have done my homework!

A few days after ingesting the capsules, my child was functioning as if she needed a priest to submerge her in holy water! Linda Blair (the little girl in the movie, The Exorcist) was sugar, spice and everything nice compared to how my baby was behaving. She was throwing tantrums, trashing her room—just overtly uncontrollable! I found a bottle of Crisco canola oil, made the sign of the cross with it on her forehead and prayed! I ensnared her in a crab-leg lock to ensure she complied and didn't go anywhere! Let me tell you, I've never experienced anything so strenuous....well, maybe giving birth (see what our children put us through). The next day I researched the pharmaceutical and wouldn't you know—two of the side effects were hyper-activity and suicidal thoughts. The medicine was quickly flushed down the toilet, never to be used again.

Although a medically-induced incident, I still bear the brunt of her all-natural mood swings, random whining, rolling of the eyes, and disrespect. As I've told my daughter during instances of irritation, she is to always honor and respect her mother---if not, there are consequences! I often wish one of the repercussions involved my absence; taking a cruise to an uninhabited island where I have an overabundance of food, plush lodging, a big screen television (with Direct TV), satellite radio, and a fine chef/masseuse, all wrapped into one. As you can see, I didn't mention a phone.

There will be countless occasions when I desire time alone..... not having to perform in a parental role 24/7/365. Before I was blessed with that position, I was an individual with personal aspirations, goals to fulfill, self-absorbed serenity, less responsibilities, etc. Sometimes I miss those days. However, being a mom is one of the most treasured titles one could hold and NEVER, in a million years, would I ever give that up!

DISCHARGE OF DUTY

I've just about had my fill
Of eyes to the skies and all out attitude
The major disrespect from my minor
Has sent me to my room
To ponder, to separate, to disconnect the drama
However, confusion clings to me
As a tick clutching its host
Depleting nourishment, equal to my patience
The numerous trips to the Land of Tantrums
Have mounted into a mountaintop of combustion
Exploding yet exhausting
Right now I want to travel back in time
To rewind and find my status—my SELF
Singularly, Individually
No plurals, no people, no childish children
Resigning from responsibilities
I've incurred for fifteen years
Going AWOL- Another Way Of Living
To where I'm first, not last, on the totem pole
Expectant of everything, wanting for nothing
No hands-on homework, No suffering mood swings
Unselfish slaves serving me
As I'm lax in luxury
I need time for the ME time
Before I re-enlist
And resume my position on the front lines

February 2, 2013

Having been married for almost 50 years, my parents are the epitome of a desired union. Although the two grew up together, played husband and wife at their church's Tom Thumb wedding (ages 9, 10) and developed a deep-rooted friendship, they also established a foundation of mutual love and respect. Not once did I witness intent to injure the other by way of words or actions. Mom and Dad were, and still are, a team: harmonious partners who enjoy and embrace their journey as one.

Despite the fact they've endured challenges, disagreed on issues and argued every blue moon, preservation of their promises---to love and honor each other, unwavering during sickness and overall health, whether rich or destitute and forsaking all others--- remain intact. It's immensely important to stand as a unified front when storms arise. But for some individuals, it's simpler to vacate their vows without consideration of an imminent impact.

'Ryan', a knowingly handsome man, is a perfect example. Having first met over 20 years ago, we reconnected when he was hired by my employer. During our free time, we caught up on the span of years missed. He was married with children, while I was enduring dramatic, divorce proceedings. Every now and then, via email or a random chance meeting in the hall, we'd say a quick hello.

Since he didn't know too many people in the building, our familiarity prompted him to ask me to lunch. We met and ate upstairs in a commonly frequented area. I was enjoying our time and conversation until he began to mention how unhappy he was with his spouse. 'Oh, here we go', I thought. I felt as if I was starring in a LifeTime Movie; the victim of a bad marriage confesses their contempt, the listening party's compassion is excessively overwhelming and they end up in a steamy, lust-filled relationship.

Well, Ryan did disclose dissatisfaction concerning his wife. The attraction for her had waned long ago; basically, remaining intimately unfulfilled for the sake of his children (how unselfish of him). After his emotional essay, the gears shifted towards my personal life (no surprise), the progress of my divorce and had I resumed dating. I lightly touched on the divorce, and clearly stated I was uninterested in pursuing a companion. Ryan began to insinuate comments regarding his loneliness, and how the separation must be stressful for someone like me—a newly-inducted single mom. Having already suspected the tricky trail he was traveling, I was close to shutting down our luncheon when he inquired about an affair..... propositioning pleasure. Disgusted, I shook my head with a slight laugh of disbelief. Never had I been formally asked to indulge in adultery (as if being invited out to dinner), but the audacity Ryan possessed to imagine my willingness to participate in such a wretched liaison was beyond comprehensible. By the time I finished replying to his request----- let's just say that with my selection of articulation, he quickly understood I'm not that kind of woman.

Meetings immediately ceased after the incident. He now has a new playmate....I mean, lunch mate, he dines with during and after work hours. The gossip that infested the entire office was of his affair with a married woman, resulting in both parties divorcing their partners. While carousing together in the beginning stages, the end result was visibly inevitable; body language has a way of exposing secrets. However, scrapping your spouse to replace with a newer model is nothing but a self-absorbed, arrogant act. Numerous children have to endure the break-up of their families due to two carnal contributors.

Marriage takes work. The coming together of individuals with their own ways is not an easy task. No longer are your wants, aspirations and feelings to be considered, but the inclusion of your husband/wife's, as well. Communication and compromising are key elements in presenting each person's passions and provisions. Couples must have a strong desire and complete dedication for their union to last. Your word should be your bond! Once vowing to God and each other, that only death will disjoin, every effort should be exhausted to maintain that promise.

RESPECT THE RING

Our introduction was the seed that was planted
Enhanced with glances across the room
A compound of chemical elements formed chemistry
Potentially arousing thoughts of an affair to full bloom
I, the individual in an unhappy union
To your pending challenge of a pondered conquest
These ingredients mixed together blended to create
An atmospheric realm of scandalousness
During breaks, hushed whispers across the table
Us two, the only planets revolving our earth
Skirting the tempting, unimaginable ideas
Organized, self-ordained and about to be birthed
Our initial triumphant tryst, an afternoon delight
An uninhabited island in the back seat of my Chevy
Thoughts of our families fleeted our minds
Behaving as if high school teenagers going steady
Infected with the contagion of a red-hot romance
Resurrected and revived this dead woman walking
Oblivious to surroundings outside our world
Nourishing nosy co-workers with non-stop talking
Absenteeism will never be regarded an option
Supplying my Monday-Friday, 5-day fix
Addicted to your sweet nothings, which mean everything
Cherishing uninhibited, exhilarating moments
Our illegal acts make me feel like a felon
Violation of vows I once proclaimed
Prohibited passions due to my husband's priorities
Left me detached, drowning in disdain
Parched for presence of an intimate nature

Dehydrated from enduring a desert storm
A tall drink of water quenched my thirst
Hydrating my hopes of being reborn
But all that seems well doesn't always end that way
As rumors found entry into my residence
I confirmed the conversation as accurately authentic
Blaming the spouse for creating my non-existence
A disabled marriage now demolished
Leaving me free to continue my extra-curricular
With a sudden, unexpected change of heart
To his unsuspecting family, he returned
Angry, alone and taken advantage
Indecisive of a future plan
Allowing my vulnerability to be susceptible
Has resulted in my singular stance
The woman in the mirror has learned her lesson
Dishonoring the pledge, "Til death do us part"
For the grass isn't greener on the other side of the fence
When it comes to pursuing affairs for your heart

March 23, 2014

After the finalization of my divorce and the penning of 'D-Day', I became inspired about my next chapter of life and wrote, 'Opportunity'.

D-Day was therapeutic. It allowed me to regurgitate the accumulation of disgust, drama, and contempt that I had endured during the 4 years of my "marriage". Opportunity was a clean-slate assertion that left me feeling I had endless possibilities and promise; the ability to pursue the dreams I was unable to delve into and fulfill when I was married.

I juggled an overflow of obligations as a full-time mom and wife. 'Jody' did not provide the necessary spousal support that was desired and required for me to passionately work towards my personal goals. Instead, I put my pen and paper aside to assist with his ambitions. The ironic summation; resuming his venture of selling a line of T-shirts he created after becoming disinterested.

Now that I'm solely responsible for myself and my daughter, a wealth of weight has been lifted; seizing the availability to recommence my projects. My opportunity for a brand new chapter in my storybook is now! I'm enthusiastically preparing and awaiting a life-altering moment to hoist me to a higher level than where I presently find myself.

It's personally mandatory to maintain a sense of readiness, for opportunities appear and disappear in the blink of any eye.

So, are you ready for your Opportunity?

OPPORTUNITY

There you are standing in front of my face
Just knowin' you're here makes my heart race
There's nothing else that makes me feel like you do..

You drive me..

Sometimes I see you often, then sometimes I don't
Sometimes you'll knock on my door, sometimes you won't
Never know when you're comin', so I'd better prepare..

You surprise me..

You rise like dough when yeast activates
If I don't pursue, you'll abandon with haste
I'd better ensue for there's no time to waste..

Don't leave me..

I've got things in order, my bags are packed
Blinded by my blueprints, I look forward, not back
Anticipating a new beginning..

I'm Ready!!!!

May 22, 2006

T. Marie

I've desired to make writing my life-long companion and occupation for years; a dream that I work in hopes of becoming a reality! Even though I've had my family's support, part of me longed to apprise my ambitions and aspirations with others. Be that as it may, I still felt the need to proceed with caution. Regardless of friendship or acquaintance---even individuals whose blood runs through your veins---folks can fake a facade; portraying a front of artificial elation while camouflaging their contempt, or shaming you for "selfishly" selecting to birth your baby! Those types of attitudes can obstruct one's ability to think and behave realistically.

'Tre' Unique', a female group established in my hometown about 25 years ago, had designated 'Krystal' as their lead singer. She had the sound, the look and the style, but also two children accompanied with a live-in boyfriend. Tre' Unique's hard work produced a couple of hit songs and after their initial album, rumors circulated that the producer was launching a solo project for the lead songbird. Partnered with the luminous package she possessed within, his business sense conceptualized a formula for stardom! Krystal's career evolved to the big screen; appearing in several movies. Her roles limited much notoriety but she was well on her way to fulfilling her destiny. There was one problem...and it began with the letter, B!

BOYFRIEND! Although I did not know Krystal personally, I was familiar with her circle of friends. Come to find out, her significant other was unhappy with her new found fame. He was unable to commend her career choices now that the doors of opportunity were widening. Her judgment became clouded and indecisive from his brewing jealousy; should she continue her journey of dreams, or discontinue her destination for a drive back to her hometown?

'Justin', who inspired my poem, Life Support, proclaimed he understood the importance of finishing my book, yet attempted to make me feel guilty. He voiced I should have either interrupted my thought pattern to call him on his lunch breaks (he said hearing my voice brightened his day), or initiate tasks after speaking to him. Despite the fact my creative juices might have been flowing, the potentiality of forgetting what needed to be recorded did not concern him. The fussing about my future proved to be too much, and there was never a possibility of sacrificing my endeavors to appease his neediness. In order to preserve my purpose, he was escorted from my existence.

Unfortunately, Krystal's boyfriend was successful in securing her selection. Instead of removing him and remaining on track, she allowed herself to become submerged with his insecurities and gave up what she loved and longed for.

God has blessed each and every one of us with talents and gifts. It's not only a waste, but a dishonor when we do not utilize what gives Him Glory! What God has destined for you, let no man or woman destroy! He has the omnipotent power to provide the perfect person who will sincerely support you... no matter what!

WEEDS

I LAY IN A BED FULL OF PROMISE
I PLANT MYSELF IN LAND THAT GERMINATES
I NEED AND DESIRE COUNTLESS NUTRIENTS TO DEVELOP
TO EVOLVE FROM UNDERGROUND
IN EVERY ASPECT AND REALM IMAGINABLE
THRIVING AND THIRSTING FOR ALL THINGS
TO FERTILIZE MY SEED WITHIN
THERE ARE OTHER FLOWERS AMONGST ME
THAT ARE BUDDING IN HOPES OF REACHING FULL BLOOM
AND BECOMING A GLORIOUS CREATION
FULL OF BRIGHT, COLORED PETALS
AND A FAITHFUL, FLOWING FRAGRANCE
BUT THERE ARE THOSE
WHO TRY TO HINDER MY SPROUTING
MY PROGRESSION
SURROUNDING ALL SIDES WITH POISONOUS PESTICIDES
INTRUDING, IGNORANT DISTRACTIONS
ENCLOSING, UNCONSTRUCTIVE CRITICISM
THAT CAN SUFFOCATE MY INCREASE
MY WELL-BEING
FERMENT MY FOLIAGE
WILT MY WISDOM

BUT GOD····

THE CARETAKER OF MY GARDEN
CLEANSES MY CONSERVATORY
PERMITTING MY BRANCHES TO BREATHE
OMNIPOTENT OXYGEN

MY CULTIVATOR····

UPROOTS ALL WILD AND WAYWARD GROWTHS
HALTING THEIR HARVEST
AS I REAP HIS RIGHTEOUSNESS

MY LANDSCAPER····

TILLS MY EARTH
PLUCKS AND PRUNES MY IMPERFECTIONS
PURIFIES ME TO HIS PERFECTIONS
RESTORING THE SOIL OF MY SOUL
ADVANCING ME TO FRUITION
ALLOWING ME TO BLOSSOM

January 9, 2008

Relationships seem to be incredibly difficult for me! Occasionally, I've been told that I don't furnish my significant other with sufficient quality time. I always provide a disclaimer prior to dating: I'm in the process of completing writing projects, and there might be instances when I'm inaccessible. The immediate response usually is, "I can handle it," or "As long as we can spend some time together it shouldn't be a problem."

Yet, it never fails. Complaints of my unavailability arise because they cannot comprehend the passion I possess when it comes to my creative craft. One of the problems I had with my last boyfriend was time, but it was destined to fail before it even began.

'Justin' and I attended the same high school; reuniting via a social networking website. By no means were we an item....just casual friends greeting each other as we passed by in the halls. Over two decades had elapsed since we last convened, so I gave Justin my phone number in hopes of securing a verbal reunion. A few weeks after his call, he mentioned how he would like to see me. When he came over, we reminisced about the days of old until it was time for me to pick up my princess from the YMCA. Justin decided to come along for the ride. After dropping off one of my daughter's teammates, the three of us decided to get a quick bite to eat and purchase a few items at Bath & Body Works. We had a good time. As the weeks went by, Justin and I began dating.

Now, I'm not one to discriminate when it comes to individuals and their circumstances, but this was going to be the first time associating with someone who did not possess a permanent job (he had been laid off/temporarily not working), let alone his own dwelling. I know, red flags up already! But I sincerely liked what I was discovering, except for the employment and financial aspects. Our personalities seemed to mesh and we connected on other levels: our sense of humor, family style, etc.

Within weeks, a temporary placement company had secured a job for him with the hopes of being hired on, but he didn't have a lot of money saved prior to starting the position. I provided him monetary loans for gas and prepaid phone minutes, which he reimbursed. Even though the requests weren't asked on a consistent basis, it still troubled me. No man---boyfriend or friend---ever inquired to borrow money. Although I had empathy for Justin's situation, I'm a single mom; working and handling my own business without outside assistance.

In-between time, Justin and I were attempting to adjust to his second shift work schedule. There were nights during the week that I would stay up to see him (he 'd usually arrive around 11:50 pm.), in addition to various weekend visits. As a token of appreciation, he'd frequently purchase groceries to share with my household.

Justin resided with a cousin at the time of our association. My dad happens to own property and a tenant had recently moved out. I questioned if he would consider renting to Justin, explained his employment situation, had him call my father to inquire about the house and fill out an application. Due to having met Justin previously, I informed my dad to consider this as business....nothing personal.

The two spoke and reached an agreement. To assist with the monthly rent, one of his cousins moved into the loft space upstairs. Justin was thoroughly ecstatic; relieved to depart from his relative's couch into his own habitat. There was an issue: the home was appliance free, which neither were in possession of. I loaned them a fold-out table and deep freezer since I was not using them at the moment. Periodically, I allowed Justin to wash and dry his clothes at my place instead of frequenting the laundromat. I believe in helping others, but don't attempt to "subtly" take advantage of my kindness!

While relaxing at home after work one day, he called and asked if I would drive to his job to loan him some gas money. Regardless of stating a payback date within the following two days, the answer was a firm, NO! Enough was enough! I had previously mentioned the need for him to budget his finances; list the monetary priorities in order to save sufficient funds for the week. He verbalized his offense regarding my suggestion, but I explained how my dad had serviced me with the same advice and not to misinterpret my recommendation as a personal blow. Justin had been employed for over three months and was in negotiations of being hired on. I felt that he should have some money set aside by now.

The actual straw that broke the camel's back happened one afternoon while he was at work. I text to inform him that I was writing, and would probably be unavailable to speak during his lunchtime. I was cruising on a creative composing role, but would talk to him on his upcoming break. Justin never called during that time, nor sent the nightly text informing of his safe arrival home. I knew he was behaving immaturely, however, when I called him the following day, he refused to answer the phone; instead replying with text messages. I was done! After a week and a half of not conversing, I alerted him that I wanted the money he previously borrowed. Justin promised reimbursement as soon as possible, but I emphasized the fact that he was almost two weeks late. After a couple of rounds of arguing and reiterating my demand of compensation, I decided to sever all ties. A few days thereafter, I retrieved my belongings he and his cousin had borrowed. Out of the blue, Justin confessed his reasoning for not speaking to me; he didn't feel important because I should have talked to him during his lunchtime. I explained that if he truly understood and supported the completion of my writing, he wouldn't have heartily embraced the delay of conversation.

Some people unknowingly take advantage of the kindness and compassion of others. In my opinion, Justin did the exact opposite. Perhaps he felt entitled to receive his financial needs met due to our relationship. However, a male friend reminded me that a real man, no matter what his status, would refrain from asking a woman for money.

Truly a lesson learned! Never will I date a man who's unable to fully support himself in every way. I tried to overlook the obstacles, but they were too numerous to overcome. No more aids of financial assistance or funding monetary favors. I have one dependent to support, and from here on out that's the way it will remain!

LIFE SUPPORT

I was aware, when our under layer was laid
That your structure stood on unstable ground
Unfortunate happenings accompanied with bad breaks
No money saved...not much of it around
An extended hand and opportunities provided
Truly out of my normal routine
For everyone deserves a second chance
To rebuild and live in prosperity
A key to my city was hesitantly granted
To provide access for necessities and food
Persistently praying for a permanent job
Your "Ms. Good Deeds" desired to support you
Support, however, has various meanings
Definitions you wanted to twist and contort
Custom designed to fit your circumstances
To enable approval of your constant falling short
A sponsor of strength and endless encouragement
Were what my intentions intended to be
But your 'lack of' was limited to bumming and borrowing
Which literally began draining the life out of me
Although I was helping, you were hindering
The relationship we were attempting to grow
Steady petitions for financial withdraws
From the institution of Girlfriend, Savings & Loan
Going the extra mile, that I will do
To assist someone who's truly in need

But you're traveling to the land of Taking Advantage
Which is a place prohibited for you to be
Even though I hold the title of your woman
And our courtship has only recently begun
Does not hold me accountable for all
Your debt due from past infractions
When promises of payback dates delayed
And "as soon as I can" reasons reiterated
My hypothesis proved to be coming true
That our relationship was most certainly outdated
I'm finished funding your independent foundation
Nowhere else to go, the course has been run
Having to demand restitution before I relieve you
Leaves me feeling confused and stunned
The audacity one has to possess such anger
When asked for the return of something borrowed
Consistent stalling only made matters worse
After the bountiful blessings that I bestowed
My single household remains in first place
Whether or not I have a man
I refuse to be a financial saving grace
On your two feet, take a solitary stand
Renewing your future is an achievable goal
It can be accomplished if you just start believing
But, right now it's necessary for our paths to part
For our end is essential to ignite your beginning

September 15, 2013

I wrote, 'Suga-Free', during a time when I was striving to focus solely on my projects-- writing this book, a young adult novel and songs for a lullaby CD---while juggling full-time employment and single motherhood. Even though I was in the midst of a challenging schedule, part of me still longed for a relationship. I missed the strength of a man's caress, the tenor of his voice tickling my ears, and captivating kisses adorning my lips. Informing a person of interest that my aspirations were my primary focus always received a resounding acknowledgment of comprehension. But, time always proved otherwise.

There were instances when I'd have to forfeit outings with my current sweetheart. Because of his personal interpretations behind my voluntary exclusion, disagreements regarding my discipline occurred. I attempted to conform my schedule to alleviate his negative attitude, but ended up disappointing myself. I temporarily extinguished my passions just to satisfy someone's request. Regardless of other's thoughts, comments or behavior, I needed to take matters more seriously!

God has abundantly blessed me with gifts and talents that I want to utilize, inspire and share with the world. Recurring interruptions will prove costly to my desired career; either to the point of delay or destruction. After repeated, unsuccessful efforts to maintain a relationship, I've accepted the fact that I need to postpone that part of my life. Significant others have displayed the inability to truly understand and withstand the devotion towards my ambitions. Although I miss the advantages of enjoying a companion, I relish the drama-free life of being 'Suga Free'!

SUGA-FREE

I'm living the life of being Suga-Free
I don't want any cookies, cake or candy
I won't have to worry about the HIV
Ever having a chance to infect me
No worries from a lover fakin' a show
Or wonders if my man is on the 'down low'
Interrogations of where I've been don't exist
Getting upset about the little things, I won't miss
Putting the toilet seat down—not a care in the world
Or getting upset when you introduce me as your "girl"
A woman, I am, should be revered as a Queen
I don't have time for games—you know what I mean?
I'll give you time to grow and mature, hopefully
If we get together, then it was meant to be
But right now on my life I have a call
God spoke my name, and I'm giving Him my all
Suga will only distract my dreams away
While I'm off to work, Suga wants to play
Disciplined and determined, I'll reach my goal
Either with sincere supporters or going solo
Being Suga-Free I can focus on myself
If I happen to fall short, I can't blame nobody else
I'm Free to utilize all He's placed within me
To reach my goal of being all I can be

March 22, 2008

Don't you just hate it when you keep putting off important tasks and deadlines? I know I do! Numerous times, I've postponed my primary plans by initiating additional projects before completing the original one.

It took me awhile to resume my writing of this book. I had outlined my objectives and arranged the execution of my strategies. Passion and persistence were my best friends, for a spell. But wouldn't you know----other wonderful ideas came forth: a television show, a screenplay for an independent film, character sketches, scenes...the whole nine! After the excitement of new and awaiting ventures, I had to retreat and return to my initial intentions.

There are moments when I can be my own worst enemy! I handicap my hopes of finalization when I find myself not wanting to compose. Although I long for the chance to write professionally, I don't always take the necessary steps to pursue and achieve my dream. I know what I have to do; at times it's the implementation that can be problematic.

To remedy this ailment of procrastination, I've posted motivational and spiritual affirmations on my desk at work and in my bedroom. I need to feed myself encouragement on a consistent basis and those are the two places where I spend the majority of my days.

I only have the woman in the mirror to blame if I fail to reach my goal! I'm striving for more in my journey of life.... It's My Time!

It's Time!

Why, oh why, do I procrastinate?
Sometimes I feel I inflict self-hate
Much disappointment in my actions
Stalling repeatedly, producing no reactions
The dream is there, my hope alive
But I can get intertwined in so much jive....
Mess, playin' round
Need to keep both feet on the ground
Behave like a responsible woman
For without me, "IT" won't get done
You ask, what is "IT"?
Well, "IT" is mine
Something rare, Something precious
A genuine find
A gift given by my Heavenly Father
Gotta make HIM proud of me
So HE can see
That I don't trash treasures relinquished unto me
HE planted the seed
Now, I must sow
I've obtained knowledge to know that if I put forth "IT" will grow
"IT" will blossom, be fruitful and multiply at will
But yet, knowing this, why do I sometimes sit still?
The reward is there---just right around the bend
If I don't make it there's no one else to send
For my gift is unique...one of a kind
Please...Peace, be still...give clarity to my mind!!!
To understand that each moment and minute passed by is lost
I've not obtained the strength to surrender at any cost

Deafeat?----Not in my dictionary
Forfeit?-----Not in my word find
If I just get my priorities in order
I will always possess the time

May 11th, 2006

Acknowledgments

First and foremost, I thank God: My Creator, My Heavenly Father, and the Omnipotent Power that resides inside of me! Without You, not only would I be nothing, but absent of all You placed within me to achieve Your purpose. You've always kept Your promise---to never leave, nor forsake me! Through all of my trials and tribulations, Your mighty hand and Supernatural Favor assured that no weapon formed against me ever prospered! Your unconditional love is beyond amazing; for I've disappointed You on many occasions with words and actions. And even though I'm not worthy, Your new mercies awaken me every single morning........granting me another day, another chance! I pray that with every word I write and speak, You get the glory and praise, and others, including myself, receive the blessing! I love you, Daddy!

My beloved parents, Frank and Doris-- Lord, have mercy, where do I begin? God gifted me to you for a specific reason---He knew the two of you possessed the strength, ability, patience, and love to endure a child like me! With every twist, turn, trial and triumph, you have always been by my side, no matter what! Your numerous answered prayers and foundation of parenting, mentoring, friendship and spiritual guidance, have greatly enriched my life with blessings. Although as a youngster your lessons and lectures irked me to no end, they provided the wisdom and knowledge to produce the successful woman you call, Daughter. I love you, both!

Grannie Pearl; the beautiful matriarch of the family! You bring so much joy to my heart, with your cute self! I cherish our unforgettable memories and conversations, accompanied with prolonged periods of laughter. So many times I've sought your advice, and never did you disappoint (well, only if it was something I didn't want to hear), steering me in the Godly direction, regardless of my opinion. Appreciative of our hands-on relationship since birth, I've relished you being one of the prime parental figures in my life, in addition, becoming one of my best friends! I love you and thank you for being my praying grandmother!

Jalyn, my lovely daughter! Throughout the years we've sustained plenty of life's storms, but successfully weathered them together! You are the miracle that matured me in my time of need; intensifying my desire to recommence and accomplish my destiny, my purpose—no matter what obstacle attempted to dethrone this Queen. You are my princess: anointed with greatness, courage and strength. As I observed your endurance of multiple surgeries, sat by your side through chemotherapy (accompanied with sickness), my admiration for you multiplied to new heights. Not once did, or have you given up, thrown in the towel, or called it quits because of your challenges. Continually, your head is held high, inspiring others in spite of your condition of Neurofibroma Type 1. The diagnosis has not defeated you----pursuing of your dreams and goals are in full effect. Remain on the righteous and positive path of life, deterring from negative people and wrongful deeds. Trust God's direction! I thank you for being my closest and personal cheerleader, encouraging and motivating me when my tank is near empty. Your love for me envelops every fiber of my being, and I'm grateful and honored God chose me to mother one of His most precious creations! I love you, Tink!

Additional Love "Shout Outs"

Thank you to my sister and nieces—Athena and Jordie, your humorous antics provide the joy of laughter to my heart, and I thank God He answered our prayers for your return home—you were truly missed! The both of you have always supported me with your prayers and presence, which are greatly appreciated. Reaux, I am extremely proud of you for becoming the first in our family to achieve your Master's degree! Your hard work and hustle will result in rewards beyond your wildest dreams. Always follow the path that God places before you---He will direct you to greatness! Love you all!

To my Pastor, Bishop Timothy J. Clarke, presiding at First Church of God. Thank you for preaching the unadulterated Word of God! I'm truly blessed to have been lead to become a member, for under your leadership my Spiritual life has grown, blossomed and fortified my soul! I love you and First Lady C!!!

Sandy B----my girl! Who would have thought attending a paralegal class would produce years of friendship? Regardless of us not speaking on a daily basis, we never skip a beat---picking up where we left off. Thank you for our talks, laughs (too numerous to count because you're crazy!!), prayers and support. You are truly one of a kind, and I love you, sis!

Joyeeta Stevenson--My baby sista.....you are not only my treasured friend, but an inspiration! The spirit and drive you possess is incredibly infectious. I am extremely proud of your accomplishments—The single-parent network, Kindred Spirits, your all-natural skincare line, Joyeeful Potions—created and operated while maintaining the status of, 'Outstanding Single Mother'! You have been a blessing to those that surround you, including myself. The best is yet to come. Continue to look and press forward because nothing but greatness is your destiny. Love you, girl!

Colleen Blackston---My beautiful and talented cousin! From our days of old as the quiet and reserved of the bunch, you have blossomed into an exuberant individual, living life to the fullest. God has abundantly blessed you and gifted you with an overflow of expressive creativity, in numerous forms. It brings me joy to witness the happiness and fulfillment from your recent "new chapters" in life, which I had the pleasure of attending one, in person! There's nothing more powerful than the support of family, and I thank you, so much, for your belief in me and your stimulating words of strength. I pray that our reconnection will pave the way for continuous contact, and I love you, dearly!

Stacie McCall Harris---the Superwoman I want to be when I grow up! From the days of old at the NYSP summer camp, you've always encompassed a competitive and determined spirit. I'm thankful to social media for bringing us back together after all of these years. I'm extremely proud of your achievements; past, present and future ones to come. Your faith-filled, motivating words rejuvenated and stirred my Spirit, and your advice has benefited me, tremendously. Having walked this journey before me, your guidance and wisdom are priceless gifts. Thanks, so much, and love you, sis!

Salsalita, Ms. Lena and Sweet P.—my co-workers from Alcatraz; your support originated from day one. The enthusiastic, encouraging words and actions lifted me along the way, and I thank you! Henrietta, Dimples, Foxy Brown, and the "D.L.", not only do I cherish our sistahood, but also your belief in me!

Mark Williams, I thank you for blessing me with your professional pictures. Although we could not use them this time around, there's always the next time! I look forward to many years of partnership. Tom Hawk (Hawk Galleries—Columbus, Oh), I appreciate the use of your beautiful studio. Also, Serbennia Davis thank you so much for working with me.

To my additional family members, friends and acquaintances, who have participated in the beginning of my journey, thank you for your contributions. Regardless of what they consisted of: prayers, publicity, a listening ear, an embrace, financial investment, or any supplemental support, your confidence in me is treasured!

Last, but not least, I want to thank the 'Anonymous Donors' who provided influential means for my book, despite motivational or malicious intent. Your performances paved the way towards instilling and implementing positive reactions, revelations and resolutions within my life that I am able to share with the world!

www.ingramcontent.com/pod-product-compliance
Lightning Source LLC
Chambersburg PA
CBHW030942090426
42737CB00007B/513